Perspectives on the Parables

Perspectives on the Parables

An Approach
to
Multiple Interpretations

MARY ANN TOLBERT

FORTRESS PRESS   PHILADELPHIA

The material on pp. 94–107 includes a revision of my article "The Prodigal Son: An Essay in Literary Criticism from a Psychoanalytic Perspective," *Semeia* 9 (1977): 1–20, which is used here by permission of *Semeia* and the Society of Biblical Literature.

In editing this book Fortress Press has been guided by the twelfth edition of the University of Chicago Press *Manual of Style*.

Library of Congress Cataloging in Publication Data

Tolbert, Mary Ann, 1947–
   Perspectives on the parables.

Includes indexes.
  1. Parables. I. Title.
BT375.2.T65   226'.8'06   78-54563
ISBN 0-8006-0527-6

7126F78   Printed in the United States of America   1–527

In memoriam

Norman Perrin
and
William B. Cloe, Sr.

Contents

Preface   9

Introduction   13

I. The Problem of Multiple Interpretations   15
   Parables in the New Testament
   Modern Research on the Parables
   The Parables as Parables of Jesus
   The Parables as Parables of the Gospels
   A Selective Historical Overview
   The Emergent Question

II. Two Models for the Parable Form   33
   Models
   A Semiotic Model
   A Rhetorical Model
   The Necessity of Interpretation

III. Parables In the Gospels and Out   51
   Gospel Setting: Pros
   Gospel Setting: Cons
   The Continuing Value of a Polyvalent Form

IV. Guidelines for Interpretation   67
   Interpretation as Art
   Two Axioms
   The Parable Text
   Narrative Structure
     The Manner of Discourse
     The Rhetorical Style
   Clustering the Parables
   The Parables and Realism

V. Example: The Parable of the Prodigal Son   93
        The Parable and Dream Work
        First Interpretation
        Second Interpretation
        Evaluation

    Conclusion   115

    Notes   117

    Selected Bibliography   135

    Indexes   139

Preface

On that late September morning in 1971 when I first set foot on the campus of the University of Chicago I had an appointment to meet my new doctoral advisor. Another beginning student and I were ushered into the office of the biblical field chairman and professor of New Testament, and I had my first experience of Norman Perrin. Looking down at my dossier and then up at me, he remarked, "Well, you, of course, will write your doctoral dissertation on the parables." It was done; my graduate career was set. My lasting regret is that he did not live to see this result of the project that he, by *fiat,* had begun. I think, I hope, he would have liked it.

I write now with the clear realization of what I owe not only to Norman Perrin but also to the faculty of the Divinity School of the University of Chicago. Especially to my dissertation advisor, Jonathan Z. Smith, who willingly took over the direction of my program, and to the members of the dissertation reading committee, David Tracy and Anthony Yu, do I wish to express my gratitude. Their careful reading and insightful comments helped me greatly. There is one other person without whose help and encouragement this project would not have come to be: Phyllis Trible of Andover Newton Theological School. She read the entire manuscript with thoroughness, offering ideas, clarification, and enthusiasm that were invaluable. Finally, my personal thanks go to my parents, Mary and Ray Tolbert, for their support during seemingly endless years of graduate study.

Within a year of each other two people whose lives were very important to me died. One was a master storyteller who taught me as a child the fascination and love of words; the other was a master teacher who told me how to evaluate and study those words. One death was a personal loss to me and my family; the other, a public loss to the world of scholarship. The one person was my grandfather; the other, my professor. To them both I dedicate this book.

March 1978   M. A. T.

Perspectives on the Parables

Introduction

"To you it has been given to know the secrets of the kingdom of God; but for others they are in parables, so that seeing they may not see, and hearing they may not understand" (Luke 8:10).[1] Judging by the varied opinions and continued controversies that mark the study of the parables of Jesus in modern biblical scholarship, we must admit that this characterization of the purpose of the parables, voiced by the Lukan Jesus, is as appropriate today as it evidently was when the Gospel of Luke was written. Whoever the "you" might have included for Luke, it is undoubtedly true that most modern parable interpreters fall into the category of the "others." Attempting to see, hear, and understand the parables, or for that matter any biblical material, in this present age necessarily involves the contemporary reader in the process of hermeneutics.

The complexity and urgency of the hermeneutical task in biblical studies spring both from the ancient and culturally alien nature of the biblical texts and from their perennially authoritative status, established by canonization. Much as one might at moments want to do so, one is prohibited from dropping a book or section of a book out of the canon on the grounds that it is irrelevant, completely unintelligible, or actually harmful in the modern age. Furthermore interpretations of texts made in the past may no longer be appropriate to the present day, for not only have scholarly tools and methodologies been sharpened and improved, but the intelligibility requirements of the age may also have been radically altered. Students of the Bible are inevitably caught in the mess and movement of history, and it is out of this predicament that their distinctive activity as interpreters arises. Biblical critics must always be profoundly immersed in hermeneutics, bridging the gap from one era to another.

Thus the primary question behind the study we are about to begin is a hermeneutical one: What can the parables mean today? To investigate this question, the parables themselves will be considered as literary texts with a certain timeless dimension rather than as historical artifacts of a long dead culture, and the general field of literary criticism will supply our major methodological and ideological foundations. Such an approach, while clearly not intended to reconstruct the message of the historical Jesus or the early church, also does not supplant or condemn traditional historical criticism. It reveals rather another option for research and exploration which is specifically designed to promote the parables, and biblical material generally, as living texts, addressing and being addressed by the concerns of contemporary existence.

The interpreter referred to throughout this study can be the trained biblical specialist, the concerned minister, or simply the serious reader of the Bible. Interpretation is that process by which we all come to understand and explain the text itself: in fact, interpretation is hermeneutics. As Paul Ricoeur has said:

> Then the term interpretation may be applied, not to a particular case of understanding, that of the written expressions of life, but to the whole process that encompasses explanation and understanding. Interpretation as the dialectic of explanation and understanding or comprehension may then be traced back to the initial stages of interpretive behavior already at work in conversation. . . . It is not defined by a kind of object —"inscribed" signs in the most general sense of the term—but by a kind of process: the dynamic of interpretive reading.[2]

Any student of the Bible, then, who conscientiously participates in this process of "interpretive reading" becomes a biblical hermeneut and the one to whom this study is directed.

We will begin our hermeneutical investigation by observing a few of the many diverse interpretations that modern scholars have assigned to the parables. Both their number and their diversity will raise questions for us about the parable form itself: Why are the parables so amenable to multiple interpretations? Does the parable form contribute to this "openness"? In order to begin answering these and other questions, we will explore two models for the parable. On the basis of the information we glean from these models, we will proceed to discuss how the parables have been interpreted in the gospels and in the Christian tradition and finally how they may be interpreted now. In proposing some ways of relating the parables to the present we will be particularly conscious of our responsibility to preserve both the integrity of the stories themselves and the integrity of contemporary experience.

CHAPTER I

The Problem of
Multiple Interpretations

"Let the one who has ears to hear, hear"—so the Jesus of the parables challenged his audience in Mark 4:9. Modern biblical scholars, however, much like the Markan disciples of Jesus, find themselves in confusion and disagreement over just what kind of hearing must be done in order for the message of the parables to come alive again. What kind of ears are needed to hear these stories? Must we of the twentieth century hear with the ears of the early Christians? Is it possible in this age to hear the parables in a different but still authentic way? Or in the final analysis is it still possible to hear them at all? The history of modern scholarship on the parables reflects various answers to these questions. Most interpreters would probably contend that it is still possible in modern times to hear the parables, but perhaps not with the directness or clarity of those who listened to the Galilean teacher by the seashore (cf. Mark 4:1–2) so many centuries ago, because in the course of the transmission of the tradition that original setting of the parables has been irrevocably lost.[1] In the work of historical scholarship, represented especially by the writings of C. H. Dodd, Joachim Jeremias, and more recently John Dominic Crossan, the assumption is that to hear the words of the gospels authentically, we must hear them, as far as possible, as the first Christians did. On the other hand the work of such scholars as G. V. Jones and Dan O. Via, Jr. suggests that to hear the stories authentically may not at all require the re-creation, if that is indeed ever possible, of the original cultural setting. All of these scholars, moreover, in the course of their research have presented interpretations of individual parables which are meant to reflect their own particular ways of hearing. In reviewing the history of these scholarly studies, one comes upon an interesting puzzle in parable research: scholars who share the same assumptions concerning how one must hear the parables often present radically different interpretations of the same parable stories. Exploring this puzzle and what it might mean for parable interpretation generally is the aim of this study.

PARABLES IN THE NEW TESTAMENT

Every aspect of research on the parables has at some point been a subject of dispute, from what stories in the gospels should actually be considered parables to which hermeneutical tools are valid aids to their interpretation. For our present purposes the first of these controversial areas, that is, which stories are parables and which are not, will be laid aside very simply by saying that the group of stories told by the Jesus of the gospels which the Christian tradition through the centuries has referred to without distinction as parables are the parables to be considered in this study.[2] That some of the stories called parables vary strikingly from others of the same name is clear enough: some are long while others are quite short; some are actually labeled in the text as *parabolē* while others are not; some have typical introductory formulae such as "the kingdom of God is like . . ." and others do not. What is not clear, however, is the value or usefulness of making distinctions among these stories.

Early form-critical research on the parables exerted much effort in establishing categories for the stories, of which the parable proper was but one type. Rudolf Bultmann divided the stories of Jesus into four categories: similitudes, which recount typical rather than particular events, parables proper, allegories, and exemplary stories.[3] The distinction between similitude, parable proper, and exemplary story was one made originally by Adolf Jülicher, the father of modern parable research.[4] Bultmann sharpens Jülicher's categories and adds clarity to them. The similitude narrates a general, typical occurrence like the Seed Growing Secretly in Mark 4:26–29, while the parable proper is the narration of a particular event or situation like the Prodigal Son in Luke 15:11–32. Bultmann admits that the distinction between similitude and parable proper, though clear in principle, is often difficult to determine in practice.[5] For instance should the Lost Sheep and the Lost Coin in Luke 15:4–10 be counted as similitudes since they recount typical events, or as parables since there is some particularity in their narration? Jülicher understood them as similitudes but Bultmann seems unsure.[6]

Exemplary stories, according to Bultmann, although they possess striking formal parallels to parables, are really simple models of right behavior and not comparisons with a deeper meaning, as true parables always are. Into the category of exemplary story Bultmann places the Good Samaritan (Luke 10:30–36).[7] The categorizing of the Good Samaritan as an exemplary story has been much in contention among biblical scholars in recent years. Crossan in his book *In Parables* has argued that the Good Samaritan is indeed a parable rather than simply a moral exemplum.[8] In an exchange of

articles in *Semeia* 1[9] Crossan and Via have continued to discuss the classification of the Good Samaritan as a parable or an exemplary story, hinging
their arguments mainly on whether one includes or excludes verse 36 as
part of the parable text itself.[10] The argument over the classification of the
Good Samaritan has again raised questions concerning the value of making
a distinction between parable proper and exemplary story. Crossan has
suggested that classifying the parable as an exemplary story has blinded
the vision of interpreters to the metaphorical nature of the story and thereby to the radical in-breaking of the kingdom arising from it.[11] If categories
tend to obscure rather than enlighten the texts under study, as Crossan has
argued in the case of the Good Samaritan, it becomes a highly questionable
procedure to continue using them.

The fact that the term *parable* (*parabolē*) has been used to describe so
many different forms in the gospels, as well as in later Christian tradition,
is to some degree a natural result of its relationship to the Hebrew term
māšāl. The types of sayings and stories in the Hebrew Scriptures which
are collectively called *mešālîm* vary widely in form, from short proverbs
and oracles to longer riddles and fables. In just such a way the term *parable*
appears in the New Testament tradition to cover a variety of forms. Hence
the most useful and perhaps most acceptable understanding of a parable
at the present time is the following: a parable is that short, unified story,
embedded in a longer gospel narrative, that one chooses (or the tradition
has chosen) for various reasons to call a parable.

Yet within the variety of forms designated as parables there are some
common characteristics. The parables are all brief stories, displaying a sharp
economy in the presentation of characters/agents and plot. As unified ac-
counts with some amount of formal patterning they occupy a middle range
between longer narratives like *Novellen* and more rigidly structured units
like proverbial sayings or poetry. At first glance the parables appear to
present a realistic picture; however, the realism is just as often exploded by
an extravagance in detail and description. Further, many of the stories
employ the indefinite article ("a certain man," "a certain city"), which
gives them a marked generality in tone.

It is indeed these last two common characteristics that have suggested
to interpreters through the centuries that the parables mean more than they
appear to say. Both the presence of the extraordinary within the ordinary
and the indefinite tone of the narratives undermine the view that their
world of reference can be totally exhausted by everyday scenes from first-
century Palestine. The fractured realism and universality of these stories
have encouraged interpreters to see other levels of meaning in them. For

instance the parables of leaven in dough (enough leaven to make bread for over a hundred people) and of an altercation between an unjust judge and a certain poor woman (who the judge fears will beat him black and blue) are not simply stories about ordinary gastronomic or juristic problems. Their extravagance and generality identify them instead as stories that transcend one time or one situation to extend to all times and many settings. While the characteristics of the parabolic narratives initiate this extension of meaning, many generations of interpreters have attempted to continue (or conclude) it by reflecting upon either the message of the historical Jesus, or the complex symbol of the Coming of the Kingdom of God, or the nature of human existence in the world. The history of modern research on the parables is in fact a record of these attempts to see and describe this meaning beyond.

MODERN RESEARCH ON THE PARABLES

Since 1888 when the first volume of Jülicher's *Die Gleichnisreden Jesu*[12] appeared, heralding the start of the modern period in parable scholarship, most studies of the parables have fallen into one of two major streams of research. Scholars have chosen to concentrate on the parables either as parables *of Jesus* or as parables *of the gospels*. The source of this distinction can be found in the contributions of form and redaction criticism to biblical scholarship. Studies using these critical methodologies have emphasized the reconstruction of the historical setting of the New Testament by attempting to reach behind the present gospel texts to the traditions that led to their production.

In the hope that the parables might provide valuable information about the message of Jesus or about the concerns of the early Christian sect, form critics purged the parables of their settings in the gospels and stripped them of all possible expansions and allegorizations added during their earliest periods of transmission. By studying the various layers of material uncovered in such a process, form critics have been able to suggest possible historical settings from the ministry of Jesus and the early church. On the other hand by comparing the various versions of the parables found in the canonical gospels redaction critics have been able to develop theories concerning the communities which produced the gospel texts themselves and the theological or polemical intents of the evangelists. However successful one may judge the total endeavor, it has shown conclusively that the parables originally had nothing to do with their present settings in the gospels. The gospel writers used the parables, as they used much other traditional material, to present a particular message to their own time; they were in no way concerned to record the historical events in the life of Jesus but were presenting the Christ of faith speaking to a new situation and its problems. Hence many modern interpreters of the parables have turned their attention to the individual parable texts rather than interpreting them within the context of the total gospel or even gospel chapter in which they presently appear.[13] On the other hand some scholars have purposely focused on the interrelationship between the parables and their gospel contexts in order to understand more clearly both the dynamics of the parables themselves and some of the principles underlying the construction of the gospels.[14]

THE PARABLES AS PARABLES OF JESUS

The study of the parables as parables *of Jesus* has been deeply influenced by the nineteenth-century Life of Jesus movement[15] and the twentieth-century Quest for the Historical Jesus movement.[16] The Old Quest and the New Quest, as they might well be called, differ not so much in methodology or intention as in the degree of skepticism with which their adherents view the historical reliability of data gleaned from the gospels concerning the life of Jesus. Those involved in the Old Quest were interested in actually writing the life of the historical Jesus; those of the New Quest, however, believe that the material available is insufficient for reconstructing the actual life of Jesus, but they think it is possible to gain some understanding of the consciousness of Jesus or some intimation of his "faith and faithfulness."[17]

Many of the scholars involved in studying the parables as parables *of Jesus* have been either overtly or covertly associated with this search for reliable historical information concerning Jesus. It was concern for information about the message of the historical Jesus, for instance, that motivated scholars like Jeremias, one of the great historical critics of the modern period in New Testament studies, to attempt to reach back to the most primitive text possible for each parable. Jeremias not only determined which variation of a parable appearing in more than one gospel was the earliest, but he also purged these earliest extant texts of all elements which he considered possible expansions or elaborations added during their transmission.[18] The result of Jeremias's efforts was a series of *Ur*-parable texts, texts which, granted his assumptions concerning oral transmission, Jeremias could show to be the source of all the later extant variations. If one is willing to grant Jeremias his assumptions concerning the process of oral transmission, a point which with some good reason not all recent studies have been willing to do, one is still left with a considerable difficulty in using

Jeremias's work: the parables he constructs simply do not exist. Jeremias's *Ur*-parables are hypothetical formulations; therefore the parable interpreter relying upon them is not only faced with interpreting ancient and culturally alien texts but with interpreting hypothetical texts as well. Yet Jeremias has shown that if one wants to speak of the parable actually spoken by Jesus, one must rely upon hypothetical constructions differing in form from each of the extant variations. Surely a question must quite naturally arise at this point concerning the amount of reliable historical data hypothetical texts can provide.[19]

In the three decades or so since Jeremias's work appeared, there has been a slow but noticeable shift away from exclusively historical concerns in parable scholarship. It may well be that the difficulty of formulating hypothetical texts and then drawing from them historical reconstructions of Jesus' life or message is beginning to affect New Testament scholarship.

Recent parable interpreters like Amos Wilder, Via, Robert Funk, and Norman Perrin,[20] though still concerned with the parables *of Jesus,* have moved from an exclusively historical emphasis to a more broadly based literary one. Via's book *The Parables,* for instance, develops in its first five chapters literary-critical tools such as plot movement and characterization with which to explore the parables, and only in the last chapter does he discuss the historical Jesus.[21] The last chapter comes somewhat as a surprise and definitely as an addendum, for the main argument of the rest of the book, that the parables can be seen as autonomous aesthetic objects, surely does not require a discussion or even a mention of the historical Jesus. The book is a prime example of a shifting emphasis in parable scholarship: literary concerns are becoming dominant while historical ones, though still present, are receding. The only major exception to this pattern in recent scholarship is Crossan's book *In Parables.* Crossan, while also discussing literary theory, self-consciously involves himself in reconstructing *Ur*-parable texts after the manner of Jeremias and drawing from these texts conclusions about the ministry and beliefs of the historical Jesus. Crossan's concern with reaching the actual words and thoughts of the historical Jesus challenges the growing skepticism over the possibility of such a task and can be seen, for all its discussion of literary theory, as a reflection of an earlier period in New Testament scholarship.

Thus the stream of modern parable research that has concerned itself with the parables *of Jesus,* arising from the desire to discover historical data on the life and message of Jesus, has moved during the past century from an exclusively historical perspective to a more broadly based literary one.

THE PARABLES AS PARABLES OF THE GOSPELS

The stream of modern parable research concerned with the parables *of the gospels* is somewhat less clearly delineated than the other stream of research and is of shorter duration. Modern study of the parables *of the gospels* is founded for the most part in the development and concerns of redaction criticism, a post–World War II phenomenon. By comparing various versions of gospel stories redaction critics attempt to understand the theological or polemical interest and intents of the redactors of the gospels. Since many of the parables are found in two or three of the canonical gospels as well as in the Coptic Gospel of Thomas, they have been a focus of study for redaction critics. Of particular interest are the parable chapters (e.g., Mark 4 and Matthew 13) in which a number of parables are presented at the same time. Jack Dean Kingsbury has investigated the function of the Matthean parable chapter in relation to the intent of the gospel writer throughout the whole of Matthew:

> In harmony with the tenets of redaction criticism, our study of chapter 13 is based on the premiss that, just as Jesus employed parables to meet the demands of his own situation, so Matthew employed parables that had come down to him to meet the demands of the situation of the Church to which he belonged. If this assumption is valid, it follows that Matthew has placed the parables of chapter 13 in the service of his own age and theology, and that these parables, when studied within the context of his Gospel, will likewise reflect this age and theology. Accordingly, Matthew's Gospel itself . . . becomes the norm for interpreting the parables in chapter 13.[22]

Such studies quite evidently tend to focus mainly on the historical and literary context of the gospel material and only subsidiarily on the parable story itself. In many redaction-critical studies the important elements of the parables are their relatively minor alterations from one gospel to the next rather than their major agreements.

Two other recent studies of the parables *of the gospels* have both attempted to expand their analyses beyond the scope of redaction-critical interests. Charles E. Carlston's *Parables of the Triple Tradition* begins with a redaction-critical study of each of the parables repeated in the three synoptic gospels and then attempts to determine the earliest version of the parable and whether or not it could be considered authentic Jesus material. Carlston refers to this procedure as going "beyond redaction criticism in the pure sense."[23] One wonders, however, if this is actually moving beyond redaction criticism or, rather, jumping back behind it to the questions of source criticism and older forms of historical criticism, since for Carlston

one of the primary questions to be asked after one has arrived at the
Markan level of the tradition is whether or not the story is plausible as "an
authentic incident in the life of Jesus."[24]

Kenneth E. Bailey's *Poet and Peasant* is difficult to classify from a methodological standpoint. Bailey does not call his study redaction-critical,
though his concern with only the Lukan parables within the travel narrative
(Luke 9:51—19:48), or Jerusalem Document, as he prefers to call it, is at
base in accord with redaction-critical interests as the following summary
illustrates:

> It is our view that a pre-Lukan Jewish-Christian theologian arranged the
> material into the ten-unit pattern. The arrangement itself is the result of con-
> siderable theological reflection. . . . Luke, we conjecture, had this document
> available to him. He did some cautious editing, moved in some new material,
> and shifted two pericopes out of their original position. He then incorporated
> the edited document into his Gospel.[25]

Bailey's reflections on the editor or redactor, however, are quite sparse,
and though he attempts to outline a literary structure for the Jerusalem
Document as well as the individual parables found within it, he does not
discuss any possible intent which might have informed the structure nor
does he explain how the structures he finds are related to the interpretations of the parables he presents. Hence his study is not a redaction-critical
one in any thoroughgoing way. Bailey himself calls his work a literary-
cultural approach, literary because he tries to delineate the structure of the
material, and cultural because he compares the content of the material to
oriental ways of living both past and present.[26] What Bailey fails to do in
the work as a whole is to show how the literary structure and the cultural
milieu relate to each other, that is, how the hyphen bonds the literary-
cultural approach together. The book stops rather than concludes: he has
worked out some structures and presented some material concerning cultural background, but how these elements relate to each other or in particular how the literary structures relate to the interpretations of the material
he presents is left without comment. For Bailey it is evidently enough to
delineate a structure without attempting to discuss it. The bulk of his discussion focuses upon the cultural background of the material in the parables of Luke as gleaned from both ancient and modern sources.

In all three of these recent books on the parables *of the gospels* the study
of the parable story itself is often subordinated to or at least made to share
center stage with some other concern, for example, the theology of Matthew in Kingsbury's work, the relationships between the synoptic gospels

in Carlston's, or the cultural background of the Middle East in Bailey's. There is a tendency to use the parables to open the way for some other issue of discussion or as examples to be pointed to at the right moment in the argument. Much of this tendency derives from the redaction-critical method itself which after all has as its ultimate goal the discovery of the motivations and concerns of the redactor; the study of traditional gospel material is mainly a means to an end.

Moreover this stream of modern parable research tends to shade over into the concerns of those scholars involved in the study of the parables as parables *of Jesus*. Carlston is quite openly concerned with the historical Jesus and with determining which parables can be traced back to him through the tradition. By trying to reconstruct the cultural milieu of the first century and suggesting the type of response the first hearers had to the parables, Bailey is in a more covert fashion also pursuing the shadow of the historical Jesus. Redaction criticism, of course, does not move toward a reconstruction of the historical Jesus but in the opposite direction, toward the uses of the tradition by the evangelists and the concerns of the early Christian community. Hence Carlston and Bailey have both had to deviate from a purely redaction-critical study in order to pursue questions concerning the historical Jesus or the responses of the earliest parable audience.

Having briefly discussed these two major streams of modern parable research, this study will focus mainly on the former, the studies that deal with the parables as parables *of Jesus*. The reasons for this choice are threefold: First, as was noted above, the second stream of research often shades over into the concerns of the first. The quest for the historical Jesus is behind much if not most of the modern study of the parables, but it is most clearly presented and most carefully argued in the works of scholars who are self-consciously studying the parables as parables *of Jesus*. So while a scholar like Carlston is also interested in tracing parables back to Jesus, his work at this point is heavily dependent on Jeremias, Dodd, and Jülicher. Secondly, since this present study is primarily concerned with the parable narrative itself, the redaction-critical concern with the theology and intent of the evangelist often found in studies of the parables *of the gospels* raises issues extraneous to the major direction of our argument. And thirdly, it is in the research on the parables as parables *of Jesus* that some of the most interesting questions have arisen concerning the nature of the parable form itself and the kind of interpretations scholars can derive from that form. In order to begin looking at some of those questions it is necessary to review briefly and selectively the history of modern research on the parables as parables *of Jesus*.

A SELECTIVE HISTORICAL OVERVIEW

It is beyond the scope of this section to review in depth the total history of modern research on the parables from Jülicher to the present. Such a review is readily available in articles and books by various scholars.[27] It is necessary however to note briefly the major developments of that research in order to point out a puzzle it forces one to face about the nature of parable interpretation. A careful reader of the modern works of parable interpretation perceives a strange phenomenon in comparing them: every scholar who has interpreted the parables, in an attempt to show either what they meant in the time of Jesus or what they may mean now, has arrived at interpretations which differ, often radically, from interpretations proposed by other scholars. Equally competent scholars using much the same historical or literary method can arrive at remarkably different interpretations of the same parable. Moreover the differences often appear to be consistent with the personal theological or philosophical orientation of the individual interpreter. Let us look at the history of modern parable research for some examples.

To Jülicher[28] goes the honor of initiating a new day in parable research. The main contention of his massive two-volume work was to argue against the prevailing form of parable interpretation, allegory. He declared that the parables should be understood as parables and not as allegories. The parables for Jülicher had one single point of comparison and that point had to be the one with the widest possible application. Hence in parable after parable Jülicher was able to draw out general moral principles that, taken together, read like a manifesto of nineteenth-century German liberal theology: constancy in prayer (the Friend at Midnight, Luke 11:5–8); one salvation for all men (Laborers in the Vineyard, Matt. 20:1–16); an act of love is the most important duty of men (Good Samaritan, Luke 10:29–36).[29] Later parable interpreters, while following Jülicher's distinction between parable and allegory, severely criticized the orientation of his interpretations which aligned them so closely with the theological currents of his day.

The next major step in parable interpretation came with the publication in 1936 of Dodd's *The Parables of the Kingdom.* Dodd accepted Jülicher's distinction between parable and allegory, but thought that to interpret the parables properly they had to be seen in the context of Jesus' major teaching, the coming of the kingdom of God. The first half of Dodd's book argues that the nature of Jesus' eschatological message was clearly a "realized" eschatology. The second part of the book sets the parables of Jesus in the context of such a realized eschatology and, so doing, finds that they indeed support that understanding of the message of Jesus. Jeremias was deeply impressed by Dodd's arguments for setting the parables of Jesus within the general context of Jesus' eschatological message, but he disagreed with Dodd's definition of that eschatology. For Jeremias, Jesus' eschatology was not a realized eschatology but an eschatology in the process of being realized, that is, established in the present but fulfilled in the future. It is striking, considering the nature of the question we are examining, to compare the interpretations of Dodd and Jeremias concerning the same parable. Because of their a priori view of the eschatological orientation of Jesus' message they interpret the same parable, using basically the same historical method, in quite different ways. Dodd, with his view of realized eschatology, sees the parable of the Seed Growing Secretly (Mark 4:26–29) as presenting in its description of the final harvest the present crisis in which the hearers of the words of Jesus find themselves. The harvest time is at hand, the time of waiting is over, and all depends on their present decision about Jesus:

> We know that Jesus regarded his work as the fulfilment of the work of the prophets, and that he saw in the success of John the Baptist a sign that the power of God was at work. Thus the parable would suggest that the crisis which has now arrived is the climax of a long process which prepared the way for it.[30]

Jeremias, with his view of an eschatology in the process of being realized, discusses the parable under the heading of "The Great Assurance" and prefers to call it the "parable of the Patient Husbandman" rather than the Seed Growing Secretly. For him it is not a call to a present crisis but rather an assurance that God's hour will come in the future:

> Consider the husbandman, says Jesus, who patiently awaits the time of harvest. So, too, God's hour comes unimpeded. He made the decisive beginning, the seed has been sown. He leaves nothing undone . . . His beginning ripens to its fulfilment. Til then it behoves man to wait in patience and not to try and anticipate God, but in full confidence to leave everything to him.[31]

Patient assurance on the one hand and imminent crisis on the other give to the same parable extremely different meanings. Dodd and Jeremias are using essentially the same historical-critical method; they are both interested in understanding what the parables meant in the time of Jesus; and they both agree that interpreting the parables in the light of Jesus' eschatology is the right way to arrive at that goal. However, because they each formulate the eschatological message of Jesus in slightly different terms their interpretations of the same parable diverge radically. Apparently the parable of the Seed Growing Secretly, at least, is remarkably sensitive to changes in the context of interpretation. Small shifts in the eschatological background against which the parable is being reviewed are capable of radically altering the interpretations of it. Yet, granted their assumptions concerning the eschatology of Jesus, both Dodd and Jeremias have made what certainly appear to be equally valid interpretations of the parable.[32]

While we are at the point of discussing Jeremias's contribution to parable scholarship it is necessary to deviate momentarily from our line of argument to point out two of the weakest links in the study of the parables as parables *of Jesus:* hypothetical texts, which we mentioned briefly above, and the banishment of allegory. As was noted earlier in this chapter, Jeremias developed a rigorous historical-critical method for purging the parables of any expansions or additions they might have gained in the course of transmission. He formulated ten "laws of transformation" which he could use to search each parable text for extraneous elements:

1. The translation of the parables into Greek involved an inevitable change in their meaning.
2. For the same reason representational material is occasionally "translated."
3. Pleasure in the embellishment of the parables is noticeable at an early date.
4. Occasionally passages of Scripture and folk-story themes have influenced the shaping of the material.
5. Parables which were originally addressed to opponents or the crowd have in many cases been applied by the primitive church to the Christian community.
6. This led to an increasing shift of emphasis to the hortatory aspect, especially from the eschatological to the hortatory.
7. The primitive church related the parables to its own actual situation, whose chief features were the missionary motive and the delay of the Parousia; it interpreted and expanded them with these factors in view.
8. To an increasing degree the primitive church interpreted the parables allegorically with a view to their hortatory use.
9. The primitive church made collections of parables, and fusion of parables took place.
10. The primitive church provided the parables with a setting, and this often produced a change in the meaning; in particular, by the addition of generalizing conclusions, many parables acquired a universal meaning.[33]

By removing any traces of material influenced by these ten laws, Jeremias thought he could arrive at "the actual living voice of Jesus."[34] In reality what this task accomplished was the creation of a set of hypothetical texts which, though certainly not representing the voice of the evangelists or the primitive church, could also not be proven to represent the voice of the historical Jesus. When Jeremias went about interpreting these hypothetical parables, he found that they could be classified under headings that came straight out of German Lutheran piety, his own theological background: Now Is the Day of Salvation, God's Mercy for Sinners, The Great Assurance, It May Be Too Late, The Challenge of the Hour. Recent scholars, while discarding Jeremias's classification system, have for the most part retained his reconstructions of the *Ur*-parable texts.[35] This use of hypothetical texts remains a thorny issue in parable research. As long as the aim of study is the message of the historical Jesus such hypothetical formulations are perhaps unfortunate but necessary. However, if this historical concern is not predominant, the justification for using such texts is undercut. For one attempting a literary study of the parables it would seem to be a far sounder practice to use extant versions of the parables to the fullest degree possible.

One of the elements Jeremias postulated to be the work of the primitive Christian community was allegory (law number 8). Allegory has been dogmatically and unanimously rejected in parable scholarship since the time of Jülicher. In the nineteenth century biblical scholars like Jülicher reacted totally and dramatically against the excesses and abuses of allegorical interpretation. Their response was necessary and important during their own day to correct the growing abuses of an interpretive system whose time had long since past.[36] Unfortunately, however, their repudiation threw out not only fanciful allegorical interpretations but also the very concept allegory, and their view has been repeated by scholars ever since with very little if any rethinking of the issue. Jülicher drew his distinction between parable and allegory from Aristotle's *Rhetoric*,[37] calling it a difference between authentic (*eigentliche*) and inauthentic (*uneigentliche*) language. A simile is an example of authentic language because the comparison is clear and not hidden, while a metaphor is an example of inauthentic language because it hides its meaning. For Jülicher allegory arises from an extended metaphor, while parable arises from an extended simile. The whole foundation upon which Jülicher originally built his distinction has crumbled, but his distinction itself still reigns. Crossan in his recent book on the parables refers to Jülicher's distinction with approval, seeing his own discussion of metaphor and allegory as essentially a reconfirmation of Jülicher's contention.[38] However, for Crossan parable is metaphor (for Jülicher allegory was metaphor and parable was simile) and metaphor creates "participation [which] precedes information."[39] Allegory, on the other hand, for Crossan results from that type of figurative language in which information is illustrated so that "information precedes participation."[40] Metaphor, a pejorative term for Jülicher, has become the dynamic mainspring of recent studies on the parables. One only wishes that biblical scholars would allow allegory some of that same transforming freedom.[41] The delicate and skillful blending of the allegorical and literal levels which marked the greatest literary allegories of the medieval and Renaissance period surely do not reflect a degraded, stilted, and inauthentic medium. That some of the parables too could contain allegorical elements does not automatically mark them as inferior literary productions. Literary-critical investigations of the parables may in fact actually benefit from recent theoretical discussions of allegory just as they have from such discussions of metaphor.[42] Hence the time to recall allegory from the exile imposed upon it by such scholars as Jülicher, Jeremias, and Crossan has come. Like the use of literary criticism itself, a revised understanding of allegory can open previously closed doors for interpretation.

The next distinct step in parable research came in the United States when Amos Wilder in his little book *Early Christian Rhetoric: The Language of the Gospels*[43] took seventeen pages to introduce the whole area of literary criticism into the study and discussion of the parables.[44] Literary criticism promised not only to aid in understanding the parables of the first century but also to help in translating the parables into patterns applicable to the twentieth century as well. As Jones put it: *"Only when treated as art and not in the first place as an instrument or weapon of warfare . . . has the parable a word to say to other generations than that to which it was addressed."*[45] Wilder's insights were followed up by Funk in a chapter on parable as metaphor in his book *Language, Hermeneutic, and the Word of God.*[46] The major American contribution to parable research from the standpoint of literary criticism however has been Via's book *The Parables: Their Literary and Existential Dimension.*[47]

Via takes as his organizing factor the upward (comic) or downward (tragic) movement of the plot and analyzes each narrative parable on the basis of these and other accepted canons of literary criticism. He views the parables as aesthetic objects, unified wholes that are fully self-contained and autonomous. Despite his position on this latter point he finds it necessary to place the parables in some kind of context in order to interpret them. He chooses as his context not the message of Jesus but contemporary existentialism. In this choice he is following the work of Jones, who also attempted to illuminate the wider meaning of some of the parables by studying them within the context of existential concerns. Both Jones and Via work out extended theological-existential interpretations of the parable of the Prodigal Son, but their conclusions are quite different. For Jones the parable suggests the "cosmic anguish" of existence which may occasionally be transmuted by reconciliation:

In this parable there is no logical contradiction between the suffering of the estranged, lost boy and the welcoming, reconciling affection of his father, both experiences being included, as it were, in a comprehensive human anguish which united father and son. May it not be, too, that man and God are not separated by the polarity of divine love and human suffering, but united in a cosmic anguish, . . . which engulfs God as well as man? God's giving his "only Son" implies the anguish of God: the anguish of one who longs to rescue his son from the consequences of human evil but because of his self-limitation either cannot or will not.[48]

For Via the clear emphasis in the story is the alteration in self-understanding experienced by the prodigal son as a result of the father's radical forgiveness:

The son did take the initiative to come back, but the situation into which he came was qualitatively different, of a different dimension, from what he expected. This suggests that natural man's legalistic understanding of the divine-human relationship is shattered only by the unexpected event of forgiveness which comes to him from beyond himself. Thus we may say . . . that the Prodigal Son makes clear that the fatherhood of God can be understood only as an event which now happens, as a miracle. When God is known as forgiver, he is near and no longer remote.[49]

Does an existential-theological interpretation of this parable, and particularly of the relationship between the father and the prodigal son in it, suggest the "cosmic anguish" of divine-human relations or the radical forgiveness and freedom of those relations? Clearly it does both. Investigations of the parable using essentially the same interpretive context can produce strikingly different interpretations of it. Yet, again, granted their existential assumptions, both explications of the Prodigal Son appear to be valid interpretations of that parable.

Via himself has articulated a further interpretation of the Prodigal Son based on Jungian psychology. In this interpretation the relationship between the prodigal and the father is one of the Jungian ego searching for its own consciousness and independence from the archetype of the Self: "The younger son leaves home because the ego must separate from the Self in order to achieve consciousness. But dissociation leads to alienation as is reflected in the son's sense of having sinned against his father (Self)."[50] This alienation leads ultimately to a reintegration of the ego and the Self in the Jungian perspective by coming to terms with the shadow (elder brother), just as the prodigal's departure leads ultimately to his return home.

Via and Crossan exchanged articles in *Semeia* 1 concerning a structuralist interpretation of the Good Samaritan.[51] Though they both attempt an *actantiel* analysis along the lines developed by A.-J. Greimas,[52] not only do they propose different forms for the fundamental grid of the story but they also disagree radically on the final view of its purpose. For Via structuralist analysis shows conclusively that the Good Samaritan is an example story, lacking "semantic distance and tension between the divine and the human" characteristic of parables as metaphors of the kingdom of God.[53] For Crossan structuralist analysis, with a slight alteration in the textemes studied, shows just as conclusively that the Good Samaritan is indeed a parable of the kingdom.[54] Again, the same method used on the same parable results in different interpretations, though in this particular case the method used may be as much of a problem as the nature of the parable form itself.[55]

THE EMERGENT QUESTION

These few examples from the recent history of parable scholarship could be multiplied significantly. They suffice to show that the existence of various acceptable interpretations for the same parable is not dependent upon the use of one particular type of method. Historical-critical interpretations, existential-theological interpretations, literary-critical interpretations, and even Greimasian-structuralist interpretations bear witness to the same phenomenon: competent scholars using essentially the same methods can apparently arrive at equally valid, though different, interpretations of the same parable. The differences often seem to be at least partially related to the characteristic presuppositions or views of the individual interpreter which influence his or her application of general methodological principles. The observation of this phenomenon in parable research leads to two alternative, though not mutually exclusive, logical conclusions: first, the parable form itself must in some way be open to multiple interpretations in order for so many different scholars to arrive at so many diverse interpretations, and second, the diverse interpretations are not all equally valid and a metacritical system must be employed to judge between competing interpretations in order to establish the correct one. No such metacritical system exists at this time, and whether one is even theoretically possible, much less desirable, is not a debate we wish to enter. For the purposes of this study it is sufficient to note that the state of the discipline prohibits a full discussion at present of the second alternative. It is possible however to explore the first alternative, the openness of the parable form itself to multiple interpretations, and it is to this task that Chapter II is devoted.

Our brief overview has shown that in the practice of modern parable research, even when the same method is being employed, any individual parable is capable of having a variety of equally valid interpretations, depending upon the characteristic interests of the interpreter. If this phenomenon is traced to the parable form itself, how can its openness to multiple interpretations be explained or examined? For some possible theoretical explorations of that question let us turn to the next chapter.

Two Models
for the Parable Form

"What is the kingdom of God like? And to what shall I compare it?" (Luke 13:18). The Jesus of the gospels answered his question by relating a parable to those listening. Parables themselves, however, in many ways were and are as much a puzzle to understanding as "the kingdom of God." Indeed we might well ask, "What is the parable like? And to what shall we compare it?"

In the last chapter we focused upon the appearance of multiple interpretations in the parable scholarship of the last century, even that scholarship employing the same methodological principles. Each interpreter arrived at interpretations of the parables that differed significantly from those of every other interpreter, whether or not they were members of the same critical school. This phenomenon of multiple interpretations is apparently independent of the type of method used: historical criticism, literary criticism, structuralism are all affected. It is independent of the cultural context of the interpreter: German, English, and American scholars are equally represented. It is independent of the period or time of scholarship: multiple interpretations can be attested from the earliest periods of modern biblical study to the most recent work of the Society of Biblical Literature's Parable Seminar. And perhaps a little surprisingly, it is independent of the literary sensitivity and focus of the interpreter. While one might want to argue that multiple interpretations are the result of studies basically insensitive to the literary character of the text, studies that might for example omit parts of the parable story and thereby arrive at differing interpretations of it, such an argument would find no support in the history of parable research. Multiple interpretations are just as evident in the works of literary critics like Dan O. Via, Jr. and John Dominic Crossan as they are in the works of other scholars who display no aesthetic concerns.

We noted at the end of the last chapter that the omnipresence of multiple interpretations suggests two not necessarily exclusive conclusions: first, that the parable form itself must in some way be open to multiple interpretations, and second, that a metacritical system is required to adjudicate among competing interpretations in order to determine which one is the correct reading.[1] In regard to the latter, whether or not such a metacritical system is a theoretical possibility, it is not at the present time a practical reality. Exploration of the former conclusion however is quite compatible with the present state of the literary, linguistic, and philosophical disciplines. Hence let us investigate this "openness" of the parable form.

MODELS

To what shall we compare the parable? Just as the Jesus of the gospels used parables as models of the kingdom of God, so too in exploring the parables it is helpful to develop models that disclose some of the inner dynamics of the parable form. The use of models as aids to inquiry has been amply discussed in the writings of linguists, philosophers, and theologians.[2] Max Black, for one, has contributed a useful distinction between scale models, or picture models, and analogue models. Both types share the basic definition of a model: "a representation of some real or imaginary original." Analogue models, however, rather than picturing the original as scale models do, are designed "to reproduce as faithfully as possible in some new medium the *structure* or web of relationships in an original."[3] Though the two models to be explored in this chapter, a semiotic model and a rhetorical model, share the general medium of language with the parables themselves, unlike the parables they come from the particular medium of *critical* language. The purpose of developing these models for the parable is to disclose, in Black's words, "the *structure* or web of relationships" that constitutes the parable form. These critical models, then, can be seen as types of analogue or disclosure models.

What David Tracy has affirmed about theological models can also be applied to the two critical models we are going to explore: they "do not purport to provide exact pictures of the realities they disclose. . . . Rather, . . . [they] serve to disclose or re-present the realities they interpret."[4] By using these models we may be able to understand more specifically the dynamics that "open" the parable form to multiple interpretations. A semiotic model and a rhetorical model are certainly not the only possible models of the parable form that could be developed. They are however sufficient to provide some direction in exploring the parable form and its implications for the whole of parable interpretation. Furthermore the study of two models is helpful in that they each in their own way emphasize different aspects of the "web of relationships" that constitutes the parable form and thereby provide a greater body of material for discussion than either model alone could do.

A SEMIOTIC MODEL

The Parable Seminar of the Society of Biblical Literature focused at its meeting in 1975 on the parable of the Prodigal Son. Three participants presented papers interpreting the parable from three different perspectives: Freudian psychoanalysis, Jungian psychology, and structuralism.[5] The three papers clearly constituted an example of multiple interpretations of the same parable, though the three participants were employing different critical methods. Susan Wittig, herself a literary critic in the English Department of the University of Texas, was asked to respond to the three readings of the parable. Rather than criticizing directly each of the interpretations, she chose to focus upon the parable form itself in order to develop a model for its apparent ability to generate multiple meanings: "The problem I would like to pose here is the task of understanding how a text, generated by one single deep structural pattern, can have multiple, often apparently contradictory meanings—that is, how a text can be *plurisignificant* or *polyvalent*."[6] A polyvalent or plurisignificant text is one that is open to multiple interpretations. We have seen in the last chapter the degree to which the parables fit this conception. Wittig presents a model, disclosing the nature of this plurisignificative process in the parables, from the theory of semiotics.

Semiotics, first expounded by Ferdinand de Saussure, can be defined as "the study of the sign and the sign system, within the context of its production, its performance, and its reception."[7] Saussure himself directed his work toward establishing linguistics as a scientific, systematic study of the structural and functional aspects of language. Semiotics however was to be a broader study, of which linguistics would form only a part.[8] The social function of the "whole human system of meaningful signs" was the subject of semiotic theory as Saussure envisioned it. Structuralism as developed in the work of Claude Lévi-Strauss, Roland Barthes, Roman Jakobson, A.-J. Greimas, and others might also be seen as but one aspect of semiotics, that aspect which studies the relation of signs to one another in a structured system, the production of that system, and its use.[9]

The term *structuralism*, nevertheless, though intimately connected with a specifically French school of thought, has been increasingly identified with all studies of sign systems to the point where it is possible to use the terms *semiotics* and *structuralism* interchangeably:

> It would not be wrong to suggest that structuralism and semiology are identical. The existence of the two terms is in part due to historical accident, as if each discipline had first drawn certain concepts and methods from structural linguistics, thereby becoming a model of structural analysis, and only then had realized that it had become or was fast becoming a branch of that semiology which Saussure had envisaged.[10]

Though Saussure may have conceived of linguistics as only one branch of a general semiotic theory, it was destined to pervade the whole, for linguistics itself became the foundation and model for all structuralist or semiotic analyses: "Linguistics is not simply a stimulus and source of inspiration but a methodological model which unifies the otherwise diverse projects of structuralists."[11] As we shall observe later, some of the strengths and some of the limitations of semiotic theory arise directly from its linguistic base.

The sign in semiotic theory is the union of a signifier (Sr) and a signified (Sd). As Barthes expresses it, "The plane of the signifiers constitutes the *plane of expression* and that of the signifieds the *plane of content*."[12] Barthes illustrates the relation of the signifier, signified, and sign this way: "Take a black pebble: I can make it signify in several ways, it is a mere signifier; but if I weigh it with a definite signified (a death sentence, for instance, in an anonymous vote), it will become a sign."[13] A black pebble may mean various things, depending upon the signifieds with which it is charged; alone it is only a signifier, empty of meaning. When the content, mark of death or vote of death, a specific signified, influences the signifier, black pebble, the whole becomes a meaningful sign, the-black-pebble-of-death. For Wittig the parable itself is a sign, the unification of a signifier and its signified which denotes "an object or event that has (or could have) existence in extralinguistic reality."[14] This is the normal denotative, signifying process for a sign and may be diagrammed as follows:

Sr
Sd

The first step in Wittig's argument, the positing of the parable as a sign, is the most ambiguous and confusing element in her entire essay. What exactly are the signified and the signifier in the parable story? Is the story as a whole the sign or, to take literally Wittig's reference to the phrase "a certain man had two sons,"[15] is each phrase in the story a separate sign and the story itself a conglomeration of signs? Wittig's development of semiotics does not give a definite answer to any of these questions. For the purpose of this discussion we will assume that the parable story as a whole is the sign and that the single phrase she actually mentions is meant to represent that whole by synecdoche, an inference that the rest of her argument seems to support. Furthermore we will grant that the parable story is indeed a meaningful sign, though the exact boundaries of the signifier and signified within it are unclear.

According to Wittig, however, the signifying process in the case of parables continues beyond the original fusion of signifier and signified, for in her view the parable is an example of a "duplex semiotic":

> The whole sign (Sr and Sd) becomes a part of a duplex semiotic where the signified is transformed into a signifier—*designating* (not *denoting*) an unstated signified. This signified, a conceptual entity which can designate only a moral and psychological construct not directly perceivable in extralinguistic reality, *must be supplied by the perceiver of the sign.*[16]

The parabolic signification process, then, can be diagrammed in this way:

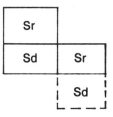

This type of second-order semiotic system is in Barthes's view the basis of all myth.[17] A relatively simple example of how a second-order system functions might be useful: One is walking along the beach when one sees a shape in the sand. That shape, the signifier, is united with the content, "pailness," and one perceives the sign: sand pail. However, as soon as one thinks of sand pail one begins remembering playing in the sand as a child with friends. Sand pail, the sign, has become a second-order signifier which is combined with the content of one's memories to produce a story about children playing in the sand. All second-order systems function in this way. The original sign becomes a signifier which designates a new signified. In terms of the parable the new signified is unspecified and moreover not directly or immediately indicated by the signifier, the parabolic sign itself. It must therefore be supplied by each individual interpreter.

The crucial element in the parabolic duplex system, according to Wittig, is that the second-order signifier and the unspecified signified are linked *iconically* rather than conventionally, as in the case of the first-order signifier and signified.

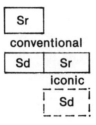

In the iconic relationship the signifier exhibits its signified, to use Wittig's example, the way a diagram exhibits the structure of its object. An iconic relationship involves an actual resemblance between the signifier and the signified the way a traditional portrait signifies the person of whom it is made by resemblance as well as by the conventions of painting. Such a relationship places certain restrictions and limits on the final signified. Again, to use Wittig's example, "The parabolic statement 'a certain man had two sons' could hardly be interpreted by the statement 'God has three kinds of children.' The two structures are not sufficiently congruent."[18] The presence of both a conventional and an iconic relationship generates more energy in the system than would be the case with stable conventional relationships alone. Since the final signified remains unstated, this energy gives the system "a dynamic, unstable *indeterminacy* which invites, even compels the perceiver to complete the signification."[19]

Besides the limitations placed on the signifying process by the necessity of providing a congruent second-order signified, Wittig notes that the context of the narrative before and after the parable, the "framing structure within which a particular parabolic sign is embedded," supplies a further intrinsic constraint on the signifying process. Though the existence of this latter limitation is not as thoroughly delineated by Wittig as the former one, she indicates that narrative context, of necessity, affects any embedded text, the parabolic sign being but one example.[20]

Thus far the semiotic model which Wittig has developed indicates how a story becomes a sign of something else that is not immediately or directly apparent. It is to define this "something else," the unspecified second-order signified, that parable interpretation through the centuries has applied itself. The semiotic model discloses one important limitation upon that interpretive occupation: the interpretation, which in terms of the model is the unspecified signified, must be congruent with the parabolic sign, for the relationship between them is an iconic one. Further, Wittig has indicated that the narrative context of the parabolic sign also in some way provides a constraining force on interpretation. These two limitations are intrinsic to the signifying system itself.

Finally, Wittig discusses the nature of the extrinsic control that shapes the second-order signified and determines what signified will ultimately be chosen:

> The second-order signified is supplied by the perceiver out of a rule-governed dynamic system of beliefs and conventions and experiences through which he finds significance in the world. . . . It is likely that the signified owes as much to the meaning system in the mind of the perceiver as it does to the signifier itself.[21]

Each interpretation of a parable, then, is the result of a fusion between the indeterminant parabolic sign and the meaning system of the interpreter. There is no one correct interpretation of a parable, though there may be limits of congruency that invalidate some readings. The semiotic model reveals the indeterminacy of the parabolic sign; such indeterminacy forces the perceiver to complete the signifying process from his or her own system of meaning, so that the meaning of the parable resides in the interaction between the parable text as iconic signifier and the system of interpretation brought by the interpreter to complete the signification process. Multiple interpretations of the parables, then, are not aberrations in methodology or logic but rather the necessary consequence of the parable form itself. The significance of the parables does not lie in some historical datum they might provide, nor in a world view they might suggest; it lies rather, as Wittig well states, "in the *reader's own act of structuration,* in his efforts to find coherence and significance, to understand both the parable and his own system of values and beliefs which is called to his immediate attention by the puzzle of the parable's indeterminacy."[22]

The value of a semiotic model lies both in its clarity and in its foundation in language theory. The linguistic basis of semiology establishes a validating sphere from which analytic tools such as signifier, signified, and sign may be drawn. The appropriateness of these tools in linguistics for the analysis of word and sentence structure enhances their value for the study of literature. At that very point, however, the linguistic basis of semiology becomes problematic. How can one be sure that the assumptions and analyses developed by linguistic theory for exploring word and sentence structure perform that same function at the textual level of literature? As Paul Ricoeur has noted, if "language is composed of a hierarchy of levels," the problem raised by the linguistic basis of structuralism or semiology "is to know whether all the levels are homologous."[23] Ricoeur thinks that they are not, and the notable failure of structuralist literary, and particularly poetic, criticism seems to substantiate his view.[24] If a linguistically based semiology or structuralism has thus far failed to provide convincing literary or poetic criticism, it may be that its value for literary study lies elsewhere. Jonathan Culler asserts that "linguistics does not provide a discovery procedure" which will yield correct results automatically, nor can linguistics be equated with hermeneutics, for "it does not discover what a sequence means or produce a new interpretation of it." What linguistics can do however is "to determine the nature of the system underlying the event."[25] Though linguistic description "does not in itself serve as a method of literary analysis," it may be quite a successful and "useful approach if it begins with literary effects and attempts to account for them."[26] Beginning with literary effects, the polyvalency of the parables, and attempting to account for them by use of semiotic theory is precisely what Wittig has done. She did not attempt to formulate yet another interpretation of the parables but to elucidate "the nature of the system underlying the event." For such a task a linguistically based semiotic theory is a useful and appropriate tool. Wittig's semiotic model for the parable does indeed disclose aspects of the "web of relationships" (Black) which constitutes the parable form.

To summarize, then, the semiotic model discloses the polyvalency of the parables to be a result of their indeterminacy, the lack of "direct, immediate connection between the second-order signifier and its signified."[27] It also indicates the iconic relationship between signifier and signified which imposes the constraint of resemblance or congruency upon the interpretation used to complete the signifying process. The parables require, even compel, interpretation, and their meaning derives from the fusion of the parabolic narrative and the belief system of the interpreter. Hence the parables are ever-new, adapting easily to the concerns of each new age, even each new interpreter. The changing interpretations of the parables, as disclosed by the semiotic model, are in Wittig's words "reflections of our own meaning-system revealed to us in the mirror of the text."[28]

Having explored a semiotic model for the parable, let us turn to a rhetorical one to see what further insights we might glean concerning the "web of relationships" that makes up the parable form. Whatever insights are duplicated in the two models we may well understand to be central to the function of the parables and to the task of parable interpretation.

A RHETORICAL MODEL

From the Hellenistic period to the end of the last century schools of rhetoric and writings concerning rhetoric flourished.[29] For most of that long period the study of rhetoric entailed the study of the classical "figures" of speech, the rules of decorum, and the classical literary genres or species. The work of such writers as Aristotle, Horace, and Longinus provided fundamental terms and ideas for centuries of rhetorical handbooks. But the rhetorical schools as schools of literary study, under increasing attack by exponents of the Romantic movement and later the expressionist movement, had essentially died out by the end of the nineteenth century. Only recently have some of the classical "figures" or tropes aroused renewed interest among literary critics and philosophers. The classical trope metaphor has in particular been the focal point of current critical discussion, a discussion that has expanded the scope of metaphor far beyond its classical background.[30] Relatively early in the modern period of parable research, C. H. Dodd defined the parable as "a metaphor or simile drawn from nature or common life."[31] Consequently the parable as metaphor has been a constant theme in parable scholarship, receiving its first full elaboration by Robert Funk in his book *Language, Hermeneutic, and the Word of God.* Thus it is appropriate to choose a critical theory of metaphor, in this instance that developed by Philip Wheelwright, to supply the material for a rhetorical model of the parable form.[32]

The precise relationship between parable and metaphor poses again the difficult issue of the hierarchical levels of language and whether or not they are homologous. To say that a parable *is* a metaphor is to suppose that one can shift from the normal sentence level of the trope metaphor to the discourse level of the parable without alterations in function, structure, and meaning. To say that a parable is an extended metaphor does not solve the problem; it only names it. What is entailed in the extension of a sentence trope to the level of story?[33] That the exact equation of parable and metaphor in some scholarship has led to both unfounded assertions and exaggerated claims of power for the parables is easy to document.

A recent example of both problems can be found in Sallie TeSelle's *Speaking in Parables.* Since, according to TeSelle, "metaphors cannot be 'interpreted'—a metaphor does not *have* a message, it *is* a message," the parables similarly cannot be interpreted. Furthermore not only do we not interpret the parables but in fact they interpret us.[34] Leaving aside the logical difficulty of understanding how a text may be said to interpret a human being, we can observe that TeSelle's own discussion of the parables indicates very clearly that she herself interprets them. In her discussion of the parable of the Wedding Feast (Matt. 22:1–10) she concludes that the "new insight of the parable is in being brought to see that everyday situation—the wedding feast and its guest list—in a new way: invitation not by merit but by a gracious lack of concern about merit."[35] Where in the parable story itself is this graciousness found? The narrative states very plainly the king's reason for discarding the first group of guests and sending his servants out for another: "The king was angry" (Matt. 22:7). Actually in terms of the story the king's action in bringing in crowds from the streets, after he had ordered the destruction of the first group invited, could be more accurately described as adding insult to injury rather than displaying "a gracious lack of concern about merit." These comments are not intended to say that TeSelle's view of grace within the parable is necessarily wrong, but rather that it *is* an *interpretation* of the story, using the themes of traditional Christianity. Hence the equating of parable and metaphor in TeSelle's work leads to the unfounded, and in fact untenable, assertion that one cannot interpret the parables. One can; indeed, one must. It is a serious deception to believe or assert that one's reading of a parable is only what the parable itself says and not an interpretation of it. Such deceptions can lead to a rigidity and dogmatism that fundamentally violate the open-ended nature of the parable form, a nature which the descriptive term "metaphorical" was originally intended to convey.

Exaggerated claims of power for the parables are present in much current scholarship, but since we have begun with TeSelle's work let us continue to examine it for this difficulty as well. TeSelle states that the parables are metaphorical at all levels of experience, "in language, in belief, in life." This metaphorical "being" of the parables

> is a way of believing and living that initially seems ordinary, yet is so dislocated and rent from its usual context that, if the parable "works," the spectators become participants, not because they want to necessarily or simply have "gotten the point" but because they have, for the moment, "lost control" or as the new hermeneuts say, "been interpreted." The secure, familiar everydayness of the story of their own lives has been torn apart; they have seen another story—the story of a mundane life like their own moving by a different "logic," and they begin to understand (not just with their heads) that another way of believing and living—another context or frame for their lives—might be a possibility *for them*.[36]

This kind of inflated language about the parables grants to them a power which very few individuals or societies, much less literary texts, have ever held. Such language may be in the case of the parables a result of confusing the speaker with that which is spoken. That a charismatic teacher, as the Jesus of the gospels is, could add power, dynamic emotion, and excitement to the teasing, puzzling quality of the parable stories is quite believable. That these stories qua stories, however, have the inevitable ability to force hearers to lose control of themselves is rather unbelievable. It would be difficult to document cases of people who in reading a parable or having it read to them experienced in that moment their lives being "torn apart."[37] Parable interpreters may in the process of working with the text find that it teases or intrigues the mind into meaningful insight, or they may find that it does not. Such insight, if it occurs, results from the interaction of text and interpreter and not from the domination of either one by the other. The "openness" of the parable form may allow the stories to come to vibrant life in the hands of a dynamic interpreter, but it may just as easily allow them to recede into terminal dullness in the hands of a different type of person. Thus we must beware making exaggerated claims of power for the parable stories qua stories, whether or not they are viewed as metaphorical in nature.

It may be true that a metaphor with its immediate focus and force cannot be interpreted, and it may also be true that metaphorical language creates new worlds, breaks the bounds of rationality, and expands the horizons of understanding. It does not follow, however, that a parable, which is a story, a narrative with characters, actions, and a definite time dimension, displays those same qualities. In fact as we saw in the brief illustrations above, parables often do *not* display those qualities. Therefore it is clear that equating parable and metaphor raises some extremely difficult questions concerning the shift from the normal sentence level of the trope metaphor to the level of narrative. It cannot be assumed that a rhetorical device defined and used on one semantic level can be moved to another semantic level without alterations in function and meaning.

Yet having acknowledged the dangers, limitations, and problems involved in identifying parable with metaphor, one is still required to observe that some relationship between the two does exist. Parables, like metaphors, are comparisons; however, while the comparison element in the metaphor is most often expressed in a single image, the comparison element in the parable arises from the total configuration of the story. Furthermore parables, like metaphors, are comparisons of a lesser known element with a better known element (I. A. Richards's "tenor" and "vehicle"); however, while both elements are explicitly present in most metaphors (in the sentence "He is a lion" both "he" and "lion," the compared elements, are given), most parables express solely the better known element, the parable story itself, and at best point only vaguely and ambiguously toward that element with which the comparison is being made.[38] How then are we to delineate the relationship between parable and metaphor? Although it is not accurate to say that a parable is a metaphor, and saying that it is an extended metaphor only muddies the waters, it is true that a parable at its semantic level functions similarly in many ways to a metaphor at its level. Thus metaphor becomes an appropriate *model* to help illuminate and disclose the "web of relationships" that constitutes the parable. Metaphor does not provide an exact picture of a parable, but it can be viewed as an analogue to a parable: it functions on its semantic level in a way that corresponds to what we can observe concerning the functioning of a parable at the level of story. Let us then explore Wheelwright's theory of metaphor as an analogue model for the parable.

In his 1962 study entitled *Metaphor and Reality* Wheelwright explored in depth the processes and functions of metaphor.[39] He determined that most metaphors could be characterized by the combination of two elements: epiphor and diaphor. These terms describe the two movements of metaphoric activity, the outreaching and the combining. Though Wheelwright asserts that both these movements are always joined in every metaphor, for the purpose of investigation they may be separated and examined singly. Epiphor is the commonly described element of metaphor, the expression of a similarity between something relatively well known and something known less well. It is the transference or comparison aspect of metaphor that allows for "the outreach and extension of meaning through comparison." Diaphor, though equally important in many metaphors, is less often noticed or described. It is the juxtapositional aspect of metaphor that combines particulars of experience to allow for "the creation of new meaning by juxtaposition and synthesis."[40] If we use this analysis of metaphor as a model for the parable, it discloses two movements in the parable, an epiphoric-type movement that builds within the story an implied comparison, and a diaphoric-type movement that combines the narrative by juxtaposition and synthesis with its immediate context, whatever that may be. Exploring in more detail the epiphoric and diaphoric aspects of metaphor may delineate more clearly the "web of relationships" that determines the parable form.

Epiphor is that element of metaphor that we most often identify with it: the comparison. Basically, epiphor expresses a similarity between something known relatively well, or the vehicle, and something known less well, or the tenor. Usually, according to Wheelwright, the tenor, though known less well, is of greater value or worth than the vehicle. For instance in the metaphor "God the Father," which is essentially pure epiphor, the term "Father" is the semantic vehicle; it provides a relatively well known concept of less value than the semantic tenor "God" to use as the basis of comparison. Although epiphor, being a comparison, presupposes some similarity between vehicle and tenor, that similarity need not be obvious or explicit. In fact Wheelwright asserts that an "obvious resemblance would not provide any energy-tension; a steno-statement of comparison is not an epiphor." The best epiphors "call light attention to similarities not readily noticed."[41]

The parable, like the epiphoric aspect of metaphor, develops a comparison, but in the parable the comparison is implied rather than explicit. Epiphor is the combination of vehicle and tenor, but in the parable only the vehicle, the story itself, is presented. The tenor of the epiphoric-type movement in the parable is left unstated and unsupplied. The need to complete the epiphoric-type movement in the parable by supplying a tenor is the impulse behind parable interpretation. We can see clearly at this point one error underlying TeSelle's equation of parable and metaphor. The metaphor specifying both vehicle and tenor may well not require interpretation.[42] The parable, on the other hand, specifying only the vehicle, compels interpretation in order to supply the tenor and thus complete the epiphoric movement of the story. We should also note that the unsupplied tenor disclosed by the rhetorical model is similar to the unspecified second-order signified disclosed by the semiotic model. Here the two models are complementary: the parables compel interpretation to complete the process built up within the story.

Furthermore an element of congruency is also suggested by the rhetorical model. Epiphor, as Wheelwright indicates, presupposes a similarity between the vehicle and tenor, though it need not be an obvious or explicit similarity. In fact the less readily apparent the similarity, the more dynamic or tensive, to use Wheelwright's term, the epiphor is. In terms of parable interpretation, not only does the quality of congruence or similarity provide a negative, limiting factor on the variety of readings possible, but also the notion of the energy supplied to a reading by the discovery of less obvious similarities between tenor and vehicle suggests a positive criterion for evaluating interpretations. More dynamic and insightful interpretations arise from the discovery and explication of a tenor with less readily apparent similarities to the vehicle of the parable story. The variety of tenors that could display some similarity to the parable story, moreover, furnishes one basis in the rhetorical model for multiple interpretations.

The rhetorical model however uncovers another basis for the existence of multiple interpretations: the immediate frame or context of the story. Wittig in elaborating upon her semiotic model mentioned that an embedded text was of necessity influenced by its context. An exploration of Wheelwright's second element of metaphor, diaphor, sheds further light on that issue. Wheelwright's discussion of diaphor unfortunately is not nearly as clear or straightforward as his discussion of epiphor. A careful reading of the section on diaphor reveals that he in fact uses the term in two different ways, although he himself never acknowledges this: one way is parallel to his presentation of epiphor, and one way is not. Since Wheelwright has suggested from the beginning of his study of metaphor that epiphor and diaphor are parallel terms, his use of diaphor to describe a function that is not parallel to the function of epiphor creates confusion in what is otherwise a remarkably clear argument.

Diaphor is the synthesizing aspect of metaphor that creates new meaning through juxtaposition, while epiphor is the outreaching aspect of metaphor that extends meaning through comparison. Epiphor is a single unit made up of two compared images or notions. The term *diaphor* also can be used in a parallel fashion to describe a single unit that relies upon juxtaposition of diverse elements to create meaning. An epiphoric word combination such as "God the Father" can be paralleled by a diaphoric word combination, one that functions by juxtaposition rather than by comparison, like Gertrude Stein's "Toasted Susie is my ice cream."[43] Another example Wheelwright uses of the diaphoric aspect of metaphor is a poem published by a leftist, anti-American writer of the thirties:

> My country 'tis of thee
> Sweet land of liberty
> Higgledy-piggledy my black hen.[44]

The author of the poem expresses his sentiments by the simple juxtaposition of elements from a patriotic hymn and a nonsense rhyme rather than by any implied comparison between the sweet land of liberty and a black hen. This kind of diaphor, the juxtaposition of diverse particulars within a single unit, is very rare, and Wheelwright rather quickly passes on to another more common kind of diaphoric activity that forms the focus of his discussion: diaphor as the synthesizing element between epiphoric units. This second way of understanding diaphor does not have a real parallel in his development of epiphor.

When epiphor and diaphor are combined, as Wheelwright asserts they practically always are in every metaphor, epiphor remains the comparison element within the metaphoric unit. Diaphor on the other hand expands its function outside of the metaphoric unit to combine that unit with its surroundings. In discussing Wallace Stevens's poem "Thirteen Ways of Looking at a Blackbird" Wheelwright determines that the "thirteen verses are related diaphorically, by pure juxtaposition."[45] Though many of the verses themselves contain separate epiphors, or what we might ordinarily call metaphors, diaphor, in this use of the term, is what holds the metaphors together. Diaphor used in this more common manner is not an element *within* a metaphoric unit as epiphor is but rather an element that *combines* units together. It can combine a succession of epiphors, or it can combine an epiphor with some other kind of juxtaposed unit. The meaning of the whole, moreover, arises from a blending of the comparison with other comparisons or with whatever other specific materials are juxtaposed to it, that which Wheelwright calls the poetic context. Diaphor, then, creates a synthesis of separate metaphors (epiphors) by combining each with its immediate context. As Wheelwright states: "The essential possibility of diaphor lies in the broad ontological fact that new qualities and new meanings can emerge, simply come into being, out of some hitherto ungrouped combination of elements."[46]

Wheelwright's study is concerned with poetic metaphors; consequently all of his examples come from the realm of poetry. It may be useful to examine a very simple prose metaphor to see how the epiphoric and diaphoric elements operate there. In the sentence "He is a lion" the epiphoric aspect is clearly present; it is the comparison being drawn between the better known vehicle "lion" and the lesser known tenor "he." What however is the function of diaphor in this metaphor? The rare case of diaphor functioning *within* the metaphoric unit is not present in this prose sentence: the words in the sentence are related grammatically and epiphorically and do not depend upon juxtaposition alone for their meaning. Nevertheless diaphor as the aspect of metaphor that *combines* the unit with its immediate context is quite evident in this sentence: indeed it is so evident in this specific, common metaphor that it is most often completely overlooked. The immediate context of this sentence is absolutely essential for the metaphor to function adequately. If the sentence "He is a lion" were juxtaposed with the sentence "There are many other kinds of animals in the zoo," then our metaphor would not be a metaphor at all. Furthermore the specific referent of the "he" is needed in order for the comparison being drawn with the lion to be perceived and understood. If "He is a lion" were juxtaposed to the sentence "John has brushed his reddish-blond hair into a thick bush around his head," the comparison being made would be one concerning the lion's mane. The most common comparison developed by this particular sentence is one of courage or fierceness, but the immediate, specific context of the sentence is needed even to confirm this "steno" meaning of the metaphor.

Diaphor, then, whether in prose or poetry, is the element of relatedness in a metaphor, the combination of the specific comparison with its immediate surrounding images, notions, or ideas. Very few if any metaphors can stand alone without a specific surrounding context to specify the comparison being drawn or enrich the depth and resonance of the images. In this sense we may describe most metaphors as dependent figures of literary language, for they always depend on their immediate, specific contexts in order to function adequately. To the extent that any given metaphor contains a diaphoric element, it is to that extent joined in meaning with its surrounding metaphors or other specific material. Common or often used metaphors like the one discussed above ("He is a lion") seem to be completely understandable without an immediate, explicit context solely because they are so common that the context is assumed without it ever having to be supplied. Such common metaphors Wheelwright would call examples of steno-language. A dynamic metaphor, or one which Wheelwright would term tensive, is a metaphor that combines epiphoric and diaphoric aspects, one that combines, in other words, a comparison with a synthesis of the comparison and its specific, juxtaposed context.

If we determine the parables to contain not only an epiphoric-type element but also a diaphoric-type element, as the rhetorical model suggests, then some of the puzzles concerning parable interpretation that we noted in the first chapter begin to unravel. For a full elaboration of their meaning the parables are dependent on their context. Hence every different context into which they are placed will result in a different interpretation. Yet some kind of context must be supplied. The gospel writers themselves, or perhaps the tradition before them, clearly sensed this demand of the parable form for a specific context by providing them with a framing story or setting. Even in the Gospel of Thomas or in the hypothetical pregospel collections of sayings where for the most part no frames were supplied, the parables were clustered together in groups, providing in effect a context for each individual parable. Modern interpreters of the parables *of Jesus* have done much the same thing. After taking the parables from their gospel contexts and purging them of most traces of their history in the tradition, recent interpreters have set their reconstructed parables in some context of their own choosing, usually a view of the overall message of Jesus (cf. Jeremias and Crossan) or occasionally a form of philosophy or psychology (cf. Via).

We observed at the end of the last chapter that some of the differences in various readings of the parables seem to be at least partially related to the characteristic presuppositions or views of the individual interpreter which influence his or her application of general methodological principles. The reason behind this state of affairs becomes clearer in light of the rhetorical model. Since the message of Jesus can be reconstructed from present sources only in broad strokes, the particular nuances and emphases of the parable context have often come from the interpreter's own personal background and persuasions. The exploration of diaphor in Wheelwright's theory of metaphor suggests that if the parables contain a diaphoric-type element, then their meaning is partially a result of a synthesis of the parable story itself and the *specific* images, notions, and ideas that are juxtaposed to it. Hence the specific personal orientations each interpreter gives to the general message of Jesus necessarily affect the total meaning that interpreter ascribes to each parable. The parables demand for their interpretation something more specific than a general reference to the complex symbol Kingdom of God or a general orientation to the eschatology of Jesus, which is all that can be provided with some degree of assurance by historical scholarship. Therefore historical critics like Dodd and Joachim Jeremias can employ the same methodology and pursue the same goal and yet end up with very different interpretations of the same parable. Their different orientations to the eschatology of Jesus form part of the juxtaposed context of the parable and are thus combined with the parable story itself to arrive at those different interpretations. Funk's suggestion concerning modern readings of the parables that the "historical interpretation is controlling with respect to reinterpretation"[47] is as we can see not a helpful criterion for adjudicating among multiple interpretations. Unless historical criticism can supply a much more *specific* picture of the historical Jesus or the particular situation in which the parables were first told, historical interpretations of the parables will diverge as widely as modern philosophical or psychological interpretations, since all the specific colorings of the historical context of each parable will of necessity be provided by the personal orientation of the particular critic.

THE NECESSITY OF INTERPRETATION

Thus the rhetorical model discloses to us, as did the semiotic model, that the parables demand interpretation. The second-order signified or the epiphoric tenor is absent from the parable text and must be supplied by the interpreter. The parables therefore do not stand on their own; they are indeterminate or dependent and must be combined with something outside of themselves. This "something," to be supplied by the interpreter, must be congruent with or show some similarity to the parable story itself, though, as the rhetorical model reveals, the less readily apparent the similarity, the more dynamic the resultant interpretation. The diaphoric-type movement in the parables indicates moreover that the full meaning of each story includes a synthesis of the story itself and its specific, juxtaposed surroundings. The meaning of the parable, then, lies partially outside the story itself in the interaction of text and context, whatever that may be.

We have explored two models for the parable form to help us understand the "web of relationships" within the parable that allows it to generate multiple interpretations. We have discovered that multiple interpretations are intrinsic to the very form of the parables. To complete the comparison which the parable story begins or to complete the signification process of the parabolic language system, the interpreter must provide some material out of his or her own experience and concerns. Moreover this material, already shaped by the personal orientation of the critic, forms the context within which a parable is read, and the parable, much like the enigmatic chameleon, combines with this context to show back its particular coloring.

Two queries might possibly arise at this point. If we agree that the parable is open to multiple interpretations, in other words, that it is polyvalent in form, and that its interpretation lies *at least partially* in the interaction between the parable itself and its immediate, specific context, then why do we not conclude that the parables should simply be left in their own specific gospel contexts, which are certainly ancient if not original and are at least clear and definite? If furthermore we are of a more negative cast of mind, we might conclude after studying this chapter on the parable form that the parables can mean almost anything. And if they can mean almost anything, what continuing value can they have for the Christian community which through the centuries has drawn comfort and insight from them? The question of the parables in the gospels and the question of the value of a polyvalent form are the issues we will attempt to address in Chapter III.

CHAPTER III

Parables
In the Gospels and Out

"He did not speak to them without a parable, but privately to his own disciples he explained everything" (Mark 4:34). At least one consequence of such a statement as this is to provide the interpretations of the parables in the canonical gospels with a certain authority. Jesus, the narrator tells us, explained all (*panta*) to his disciples so that his words and thoughts were made clear to that earliest community and could be preserved by them for later followers. It is true, however, particularly in the Gospel of Mark, that lack of understanding and sheer obduracy in the face of all the explanations, demonstrations, and remonstrations Jesus could muster continued to characterize the closest disciples, and that their authority concerning the meaning of the parables was thereby somewhat undermined by the Markan evangelist.[1] Nevertheless from the period of the early church to the relatively recent past (and for many evangelical groups, to the present) the gospels themselves provided not only the delineative background for reading the parables but also the major authoritative interpretations of them.[2] Only with the development of modern methodologies, such as form criticism and the growing interest in historical reconstructions of the life of Jesus, have the gospels receded in importance as the normative guides for understanding the parables. The question now becomes, in light of the polyvalent nature of the parables, do the gospels suggest themselves anew as normative guides for interpretation?

In the last chapter we explored the "web of relationships" (Max Black) that constitutes the parable form by investigating two models for it. In the next chapter we will discuss more fully the implications of what we discovered concerning the parable form for interpretation and research. In this chapter we need to address two issues that arose along the way of our preceding discussion: the parables in the gospels and the continuing value of a polyvalent form. Particularly in relation to the latter issue this chapter will not pretend to present any definitive resolutions but only some specu-

lative suggestions. In regard to the former issue, the parables in the
gospels, it is our purpose to indicate that interpreting the parables solely
within their gospel contexts raises almost as many problems as it solves and
ultimately fails to support the hermeneutical concern of the modern Christian community for what the parables can mean today.

GOSPEL SETTING: PROS

At the end of the last chapter we concluded that the parables are open to
multiple interpretations and, based upon information disclosed by the
models, that any interpretation determined for a parable consists *partially* in
the interaction between the parable itself and its immediate, specific context.
Why then do we not simply propose that the parables should always be
left in their gospel contexts for interpretation? If not original, these contexts
are certainly quite ancient; furthermore they appear at first glance to be
clear, unambiguous, and definite. The advantages of relying upon the gospel
presentations of the parables are important: First, they give to the literary
critic, theologian, or preacher a real *parable* text from which to work. Such
a text provides the researcher with a manuscript history as well as a clear
grammatical and literary tradition which may supply clues for interpretation. One is not required to deal with a hypothetical formulation which may
or may not have existed at some earlier stage in the transmission of the
material. Nor is it necessary to argue for criteria to be used in pruning away
stages of transmission in order to arrive at a postulated *Ur*-parable text. On
the contrary the presentations of the parables in the gospels have a real,
physical existence apart from the interpreter's skill in formulating, arguing,
or postulating.

Second, the gospel presentations place each parable in a definite context.
Since, as we have observed, an interpretation of a parable depends partially
upon the interaction of the parable text itself and its context, the specific
contexts supplied by the gospel writers limit the variety of readings that
interpreters can propose. Furthermore since the contexts are common, public
material rather than personal orientations to, for example, existentialism or
eschatology, interpretations of the parables in the gospels are easier to evaluate in terms of adequacy to the interrelationship of text and context. For
instance the parable of the Unjust Judge (Luke 18:2–5) when read within
its particular setting in Luke 18:1–8 could not readily be interpreted as a
call to social justice for the weak and powerless of society.[3] The Lukan
evangelist has Jesus draw an explicit verbal comparison between the judge
of injustice (*ho kritēs tēs adikias*) and the God who brings justice (*poiēsē
tēn hedikēsin*) in verses 6–7. As the judge of injustice finally did, after

harassment and threats, will not the God of justice do out of his goodness? The parable as it appears in Luke 18 is clearly a reminder of the "how-much-more" of God's justice as compared to that of human society, rather than any call for a reorganization of social justice within society. The point that Jesus underlines in his remarks following the parable is that if such an unscrupulous man as this judge can bring about justice, how much more can it be expected of God.

The peculiar element in the Lukan setting of this parable is the comparison of the widow's continual begging and bothering of the judge with the exhortation to the disciples always to pray. The comments of Jesus after the parable play down this aspect of the story, mentioning it only in the clause concerning "the elect, who cry to him day and night" (Luke 18:7). However, the narrator's introduction to the parable in verse 1 emphasizes and underlines the relationship between the disciples continually praying to God and the widow continually bothering the judge with her requests for justice. The narrator in fact suggests that this identity between the supplications of the disciples and the widow is the entire point of the story. Jesus' comments in verses 6–8 contrast with this focus in verse 1 by shifting the emphasis from the disciples-widow to God–unjust judge. The former comparison, though certainly part of the story and the Lukan context, is somewhat odd in that it implies a view of prayer as harassment. Nevertheless the Lukan setting of this parable, though it may be a little strange and may suggest two different directions for interpretation, obviously limits the range of readings the parable can have and makes it easier to evaluate and adjudicate them.

Another way of understanding the effect that a specific contextual setting has upon a given parable is to regard the story in terms of narrative length. The attempt to evaluate or interpret the narrative of any individual parable immediately faces the difficulty inherent in its sheer brevity. The story is often too short for the effective use of many historical-critical and literary-critical tools. In fact its very brevity adds to its ambiguous character and hence to its polyvalency. The specific context or setting within which a parable is placed in effect lengthens the narrative of the parable. The critic is thereby provided with much more material out of which to develop an interpretation. Generally, the more material the critic must take into account, the more limited the range of possible interpretations. This process of narrative lengthening is obviously not confined to the parables in the gospels. The placing of a parable within any interpretive context results essentially in the lengthening of the narrative to include that context. This formulation of the relationship between the parable text and its specific context highlights, as did the rhetorical model in Chapter II, the importance of the context to the final interpretation of the parable as a whole. And further, the more material the context presents to the interpreter, the more limited becomes the variety of adequate interpretations. Just as Luke 18:1, 6–8 effectively restricts the kinds of readings possible for the Unjust Judge, so the placing of any parable within the context of Freudian psychoanalytic theory would restrict the range of its interpretations there. More than one interpretation might be possible, but the number of them that faithfully represented both the story of the parable and Freudian theory would most certainly be small. Thus any particular context, though allowing for more than one interpretation of the parable (to complete the epiphoric-type movement of the story or supply the second-order signified), narrows sharply the range possible.

Reading the parables only in their gospel setting, then, not only provides the critic with a real parable text rather than a hypothetical one but also, by lengthening that text with a specific context, limits the number of possible interpretations and simplifies the task of evaluating them.[4] Nevertheless, though they may restrict the range of possible interpretations, the gospel settings rarely supply only one unambiguous reading for a parable. Let us look now at this and other problems involved in studying the parables solely within their gospel contexts.

GOSPEL SETTING: CONS

One argument for depending solely upon the gospel presentations of the parables is the possibility of establishing one normative interpretation for them and thereby thwarting the supposed anarchy of multiple readings to which the parable form is prone. The cogency of that argument will be discussed later. The question to be raised now is whether or not the gospel presentations of the parables really do support one clear, unambiguous interpretation. And the answer to this question is that very often they do not. The gospel settings seldom fit the parable stories completely or fully, and the gospel summaries appended to the parables many times contradict the narratives as well as each other. These very discrepancies, in fact, were one of the reasons scholars began to suspect that the gospel settings of the parables were secondary additions and not the original situations.[5] But even if one's aim were not necessarily to determine what the parables meant on the lips of Jesus, that is, to arrive at the original situation, but only to ascertain one unambiguous interpretation which could then be normative for the Christian community, the presentations of the parables in the gospels would prove a disappointment.

The first difficulty involved in deciding upon a single gospel interpretation for an individual parable is that many of the parables appear in two or three of the synoptic gospels, often in quite different contexts.[6] Since these diverse contexts influence the final interpretations of the parables, formulating a single reading that could be considered normative for the entire canon is quite difficult. Let us look, for example, at the parable of the Lost Sheep, which appears in Luke 15:4–6 and Matt. 18:12–13 as well as in the Gospel of Thomas 98:22–27. In Luke the parable is introduced by three verses concerning the disapproval by the Pharisees and scribes of Jesus' practice of receiving and eating with sinners (vv. 1–3). It is followed by a verse in which Jesus emphasizes the rejoicing of the shepherd by comparing it with the joy in heaven over one repentant sinner (v. 7). A second parable then follows which concerns the joy of a woman who finds a coin which she had lost (Luke 15:8–9). The Lukan context clearly encourages an interpretation of the parable which hinges on a comparison of the one lost sheep with the sinner who at length repents and which focuses upon the rejoicing such repentance brings.

In Matthew on the other hand the parable is preceded by a verse in which Jesus enjoins the disciples not to despise the "little ones," for they are precious to God (v. 10), and it is concluded by Jesus' admonition to the disciples that it is not the will of God that the "little ones" should die (v. 14). The Matthean version of the parable suggests a comparison between the lost sheep and one of the "little ones," but its major emphasis is upon the responsibility of the disciples for such "little ones," just as the shepherd has responsibility for finding the one lost sheep. In the context of Matthew's Gospel the parable of the Lost Sheep is a parable of duty, of responsibility for the weak and powerless whom God loves, while the shepherd's joy at finding the sheep is passed over in silence. In Luke, however, it is a parable of rejoicing over the repentant sinners, while the shepherd's activity in seeking the sheep is completely ignored in the surrounding verses. Thus by placing the parable in contexts which focus attention on different aspects of the story, Luke and Matthew have suggested quite diverse interpretations of it, one approaching ecstasy, the other approaching threat.

The parable of the Lost Sheep deserves a further comment, for it is undoubtedly one of the strangest parables in the gospels. In both Luke and Matthew the parable begins with a rhetorical question which seems to imply an affirmative answer: "What man of you . . . ?" (Luke 15:4) and "What do you think? If a man . . . does he not . . . ?" (Matt. 18:12). However, in the Greco-Roman milieu the response to the parable's opening question would be a resounding negative. No responsible man among them, if he had a moderate-sized flock of one hundred sheep, would think of leaving ninety-nine of them unprotected to go in search of one. Such an action would be utter foolishness. Joachim Jeremias, who of all the parable scholars has commented most knowledgeably and thoroughly on the Palestinian cultural background of the stories, reports, "Experts on Palestinian life all agree that a shepherd cannot possibly leave his flock to itself."[7] Jeremias implies that any Palestinian audience hearing the parable would simply have assumed the presence of other shepherds watching the sheep, even though the story itself says nothing of the kind. Some such reconstruction of the original audience's response to the parable is necessary if one wishes to continue asserting that the parables are always realistic narratives. The parable of the Lost Sheep as it presently reads in both Luke and Matthew is clearly not a realistic reflection of the actions of a first-century Palestinian shepherd. In fact many of the parables are "realistic" only in the most general sense of that term: that is, they describe occupations and situations that might be found within the cultural milieu rather than describing fabulous characters or events like mythic beasts or cosmic battles. The very brevity and lack of emotional depiction characteristic of the parables prevent them from being realistic narratives in any comprehensive sense. They do not describe the multitude of ways widows, shepherds, kings, or servants really act, reflect, think, understand, or respond. The economy of the parable form denies such elaboration.[8] Furthermore some parables are contrary to even a generalized description of first-century life; the parable of the Lost Sheep is probably the most exaggerated example of this.[9]

That the problematic nature of the parable of the Lost Sheep was evident to some within or rather just outside the early Christian community is witnessed by the version of the parable appearing in the Coptic Gospel of Thomas 98:22–27. In the first place Thomas does not frame the parable as a question to which some answer is implied. Second, the missing sheep is described as the largest of the flock. And third, after finding the animal, the shepherd reveals that he loves this sheep more than all the others. Most commentators have simply explained these changes in the Gospel of Thomas as a misunderstanding by the writer of the real meaning of the parable.[10] But might it not rather be an attempt to make an implausible story plausible? What Thomas actually does is to provide the shepherd with a cogent reason for his otherwise irresponsible behavior. If the lost sheep is the largest of the flock and the most beloved by the shepherd, then though still unusual, his actions are at least comprehensible: for this one beloved sheep it might be worth risking the safety of the entire flock. Moreover in Thomas, Jesus does not ask for or assume agreement from his audience; the parable is presented as the special action of a special shepherd rather than a common response all would have made. Whatever else might be involved in the version of the parable found in the Gospel of Thomas, it does attempt to render an impossible story understandable.[11]

The parables in the Gospel of Thomas contrast generally with the parables in the canonical gospels in that they are not placed in any setting or context from the life of Jesus. They are simply grouped together with other parables and sayings, often preceded by the phrase "Jesus said." This grouping together of parables and sayings does however provide a kind of context for each individual parable, though not as obviously as the canonical gospels do. As one reads the Gospel of Thomas through, it gradually becomes apparent that the material has special foci which begin to influence one's interpretation of the individual sayings. Such a context, though subtle, is none the less effective. Thus some parables not only appear in different life contexts within the canonical gospels but they also occur in the Gospel of Thomas from yet another orientation.[12] In the case of these parables, deciding upon one normative reading that includes all of the gospels is an almost impossible task—that is, creative harmonizing or arbitrary rulings aside.

Many of the gospel parables however are not part of a triple or double tradition; they occur in only one gospel, in only one setting. In fact a preponderance of the longer, more elaborate parables are in this category: the Ten Maidens (Matt. 25:1–12), the Good Samaritan (Luke 10:30–35), the Pharisee and the Publican (Luke 18:10–14), the Prodigal Son (Luke 15:11–32), the Rich Man and Lazarus (Luke 16:19–31), the Unjust Judge (Luke 18:2–5), the Unjust Steward (Luke 16:1–8a), the Unmerciful Servant (Matt. 18:23–34), and the Workers in the Vineyard (Matt. 20:1–15). Yet even these single-context parables often provide thorny problems for the interpreter. Some of the contexts into which they have been placed seem at odds with the parable stories themselves, and the summaries attached to them are often contradictory. For example the parable of the Prodigal Son in Luke 15:11–32 is preceded by two shorter parables, the Lost Sheep and the Lost Coin, in which the emphasis is upon the joy and rejoicing that accompanies finding something which was lost. The Prodigal Son forms the last parable in this series of three. The verse which acts as a conclusion for the Lost Coin and an introduction to the Prodigal Son is verse 10: "Just so, I tell you, there is joy before the angels of God over one sinner who repents." The context of the parable clearly complements the story of the younger son's journey into a far land and eventual return to his father's house.

If this parable ended at verse 24 where the father is rejoicing over the finding of his lost son, it would fit the context of the two preceding parables perfectly. The parable of the Prodigal Son however continues for another eight verses with a confrontation between the elder son and the father over the younger son's return. This second half of the parable seems completely out of place in the present context. Indeed some commentators have suggested that the episode concerning the elder son is not even an original part of the parable.[13] As Bultmann said: "Surely the narrator's purpose, to make plain the fatherly goodness of God, which unconditionally forgives self-condemning remorse, is already attained in verse 24?"[14] The return of the lost one has occurred by verse 24, and the rest of the parable seems superfluous. But the theme of rejoicing over the return of the lost is the focus of the Lukan *context*; it is the *gospel context* that makes the second part of the parable seem unnecessary. And the influence of the Lukan setting on this parable has been pervasive: scholars have assumed that the joyful return and forgiveness of the lost one is the total point of the parable, whether they have based their interpretations on the Lukan version of the parable or set the parable within some reconstructed teaching of the historical Jesus.[15] The parable itself nevertheless contains in almost equal parts the return of a lost son and the anger of a jealous son. The Lukan context only partially fits this total configuration and further has had the unfortunate effect of encouraging interpreters to ignore it also.[16] In the case of the parable of the Prodigal Son the gospel context has tended to obscure part of the story and thereby to promote confusion rather than clarity.

Another pattern apparent in the presentation of some of the parables is one in which the focus on the parable story provided by the gospel context is inconsistent. We have already seen this pattern in the Lukan setting of the parable of the Unjust Judge. The verse which introduces the parable (Luke 18:1) states that the story is intended to encourage the disciples in constant prayer, thus implying a comparison between the disciples and the widow. Jesus' remarks after the parable on the other hand clearly indicate an emphasis on the relation between God and the unjust judge. Hence the verses following the parable shift the focus away from that suggested in the introductory verse. The parable as Jesus explains it in Luke 18:6–7 has nothing to do with the prayers of the disciples or the entreaty of the widow; rather, it has to do with the inevitability of God's justice.

This same chapter in Luke contains a second parable that also displays, though perhaps more subtly, this pattern of shifting focus. The parable of the Pharisee and the Publican in Luke 18:10–13 repeats the contextual structure used for the Unjust Judge: the narrator introduces the parable (v. 9) and Jesus comments after it (v. 14). The narrator observes that the parable is directed toward those who believe in their own righteousness and despise others. Such an introduction stresses the theme of righteousness: is true righteousness attained by obedience to legal requirements ("I fast twice a week, I give tithes of all that I get" [v. 12]) or by abject confession ("God, be merciful to me a sinner" [v. 13])? Jesus' remarks following the parable do not contain any mention of righteousness; rather, they propose another issue, pride versus humility. The proud man who "stood and prayed . . . with himself" (v. 11) is contrasted with the humble man who, "standing far off, would not even lift up his eyes to heaven" (v. 13). Moreover in his comments following the story (v. 14) Jesus states that the exalted will be humbled and the humble exalted, but it is difficult to see how this applies to the parable, for the Pharisee is not humbled nor is the publican exalted in the story itself.[17] Thus verse 14 shifts the focus from a consideration of righteousness (v. 9) to a consideration of pride and humility. In either case, of course, the behavior of the Pharisee is disparaged, making the two contextual foci easy to conflate, but the reason for that disapprobation changes in the succeeding verse from what it was in the preceding verse.

The parable of the Good Samaritan (Luke 10:30–35) provides yet another example of an inconsistent gospel context.[18] It is set within the context of a dialogue between Jesus and a lawyer. In Luke 10:25–29 the lawyer asks Jesus what he must do to "inherit eternal life" (v. 25). Jesus replies by referring the lawyer to the scriptural admonition to "love the Lord your God . . . and your neighbor as yourself" (v. 27). The lawyer then continues the exchange by asking who his neighbor is. Jesus' answer is the parable of the Good Samaritan. In this prefacing dialogue the neighbor is the one toward whom love is directed; the neighbor is the recipient, the passive one in need. As the parable begins, the verses of the Lukan introduction encourage an immediate identification of the man attacked and beaten by robbers as the neighbor toward whom love should be shown. In the dialogue following the parable however Jesus asks, "Which of these three, do you think, proved a neighbor to the man who fell among the robbers?" (v. 36). The lawyer responds that the one showing mercy is the neighbor (v. 37). This ensuing dialogue clearly identifies the neighbor as the one giving love, the active agent showing mercy on those in need. It focuses attention on the Samaritan, who gives aid to the wounded man. Hence the introductory dialogue emphasizes the beaten and robbed traveler: he is the neighbor we are to love; but the closing dialogue stresses the Samaritan: he is the neighbor we are to be. This divergence in the use of the word neighbor tends as Crossan notes to pull the parable, which is located in the middle, in opposite directions: "In 10:27, 29, the neighbor is he to whom love must be offered; in 10:36 the neighbor is the one who offers love and mercy to another's need."[19] Again the gospel context of a parable confuses the attempt to follow the narrative's logical movement and clarify its elements.

Besides being inconsistent, occasionally the gospel contexts of the parables simply do not seem to fit the stories at all. The parable of the Workers in the Vineyard (Matt. 20:1–15) is a good illustration. It forms the end of a discussion between Jesus and the disciples concerning the rewards of the believer in the coming "new world." The chapter division is particularly misleading here, for Matt. 20:1 is both logically and linguistically (note the use of *gar*) connected to the immediately preceding verses of Matthew 19. The verse which ends the discussion between Jesus and the disciples and introduces the parable itself is 19:30: "But many that are first will be last, and the last first." As Jeremias notes, this verse represents "the reversal of rank which would take place on the Last Day."[20] Given the presence of this verse in a discussion of reward, however, it might be more appropriate to say that it suggests the reversal of reward in the coming world. That the Workers in the Vineyard as it appears in Matthew's Gospel is intended to comment upon such an eschatological reversal is reinforced by the summary of the parable (note the use of *houtōs*) in 20:16. This summary repeats, with a reversal of terms, Matt. 19:30. Hence the immediate context of the parable consistently focuses upon the reversal of reward in the coming age, "when the Son of man shall sit on his glorious throne" (19:29). But where in the parable story itself is this element of reversal found? Some have suggested that paying the workers in a reverse order from the one in which they were hired (v. 8) is the reversal element of the parable. The reversal in order of payment however is almost negligible in terms of the story as a whole, for in the end they all receive the same reward.[21] There is no reversal of reward; rather, there is the same reward for everyone, the first and the last (vv. 11–15). The reversal of reward that is so consistently and clearly stressed by the Matthean context is absent from the parable story itself. Such a context is, then, clearly inappropriate, for it focuses upon an element the narrative completely lacks.

One of the best-known examples of a parable in a problematic context is the Unjust Steward in Luke 16:1–8a. This parable opens a section of Luke on the uses of wordly goods, a section concluded by the parable of the Rich Man and Lazarus in Luke 16:19–31. The verses immediately following the Unjust Steward reflect upon the parable in various ways (vv. 8b–13). The problem is not that these verses are unrelated to the parable story but that they contradict each other. In verse 9 Jesus tells the disciples that they should make friends for themselves of "unrighteous mammon"; in verse 11 he exhorts them to be faithful in their dealings with "unrighteous mammon"; but in verse 13 he warns that "no servant can serve two masters . . . you cannot serve God and mammon." Hence at one moment Jesus is telling the disciples to make friends of money and in the next telling them that to serve money is to reject God. The context, by asserting contradictory positions, permits interpretations of the parable that range anywhere from seeing it as a serious statement of the ethics of crisis to calling it an ironic warning against the pseudosecurity of worldly possessions. The parable of the Unjust Steward has through the ages proved difficult to interpret, and the gospel context has helped not a whit.

Thus as we have seen in these examples the gospel contexts, far from providing one normative view of the parables, as often as not confuse and obscure any attempt to understand them. Some of the parables are found in more than one gospel, often in quite diverse contexts, while those appearing in only one provide the interpreter with an array of difficulties: contexts which fit just part of the narrative, contexts which are inconsistent, contexts which simply do not relate to the story, or contexts which are self-contradictory. In examining these gospel parables, however, though we have not found grounds for one unambiguous reading of a parable, we have uncovered several practical rules that should govern the relationship between a parable and the context within which it is to be interpreted, whether that context be a gospel or the reconstructed message of the historical Jesus or existential philosophy. The parable story itself is the controlling element, and the context should not violate that story. Hence the context should fit the entire configuration of the story, not just part of it; the context should preserve a consistent focus both on the parable story and within itself; and of course the context must relate in some way to the elements of the story.

Though the gospel presentations of the parables do provide the interpreter with a real text and a definite context, these contexts, as we have seen, often violate the parable stories themselves and add almost as much difficulty to the process of interpretation as they relieve. Furthermore since the gospel contexts do not record the original settings they do not help in the historical task of trying to determine what these parables may have meant on the lips of Jesus, though they may suggest, with some ambiguity, what the parables meant for certain elements within the early Christian community. More importantly, because they tie the parables to a definite historical milieu the gospel presentations often do not assist in the hermeneutical task of trying to understand what the parables can mean for the Christian community today in all its multiplicity. We suggested earlier that one reason for relying upon the gospel settings of the parables was to thwart the supposed anarchy of multiple interpretations. It is time to consider the wisdom of that argument. It may be that the Christian community today, following the example of the communities for which the gospels were originally written, needs the ability to relate Scripture to its contemporary concerns. Indeed the polyvalency of the parable form may provide exactly the kind of flexibility required for that task.

THE CONTINUING VALUE OF A
POLYVALENT FORM

The attempt to limit the polyvalency of the parables by interpreting them solely within their gospel contexts often springs from a desire for definite answers. The ambiguity and chameleonlike quality of the parables can be very discomforting. As John Dominic Crossan has said so well: "We are frightened by the lonely silences within the parables. . . . We want them to tell us exactly what to do and they refuse to answer."[22] Though the gospel presentations of the parables do not ultimately remove that ambiguity, they do restrict the range of possible interpretations, and they restrict that range by freezing the parables in situations important to the first-century Christian community.

As C. H. Dodd, Jeremias, and others have shown, the eschatological emphasis of the historical Jesus had paled in importance for many in the early church as the delay of the parousia extended. The early community became more concerned with establishing itself within the Greco-Roman world than with preparing for the imminent return of the Son of man. The gospel presentations of the parables reveal this shift in circumstances. The evangelists, or the tradition before them, were not concerned to preserve the eschatological stress of the historical Jesus; rather, they attempted to refashion the material they inherited with, as it seems to us, remarkable freedom in order to direct that material specifically to problems faced in their own communities.[23] The very writing of the gospels, then, was an exercise in hermeneutics, an attempt to understand what the material could mean for a particular period in the history of the early church. Rather than accepting as normative the actual presentation of the parables found in the gospels, should we not instead emulate this hermeneutical process? The gospel writers in their use of the parables as well as much other traditional material established a precedent for interpreting words from the past in light of the present. The settings they elaborated for the parables were germane to the issues facing their own communities, but those issues, like the communities that addressed them, have long since faded into history. The need to relate the words of the past to the present, however, has not faded. This hermeneutical imperative has engaged the talents and resources of scholars and preachers throughout the ages and has retained its force even to this very hour.

The methodologies developed to meet the hermeneutical needs of changing generations have been varied. While the evangelists actually rewrote traditional material, once the gospels began to be increasingly accepted by the growing Christian community of the second, third, and fourth centuries, the material, including the parables, became in a real sense fossilized. Though the problems faced by the church in late antiquity and the early Middle Ages were quite different from those which concerned the early Christians, the written gospels themselves were not altered. Since rewriting could no longer solve the hermeneutical dilemma, other solutions were sought. One way scholars and theologians of the Middle Ages related the traditions of the Christian faith to the changing situations of a worldwide community was by refining the art of allegorical interpretation.

Our intention is not to debate the merits or demerits of allegorical interpretation. It does serve however as an excellent example of hermeneutical activity, for it was the dominant interpretive procedure from the time of Origen to the Enlightenment. It allowed the church through all those centuries to apply orally in preaching and teaching a historically conditioned text to all the detailed and complex circumstances of existence. In the New Testament itself Paul explicitly used allegorical interpretation to adapt the Hebrew story of Abraham to the problems of the early Christian community (Gal. 4:22-31). Augustine was first attracted to Christianity by the eloquent allegorical interpretations he heard in the preaching of Ambrose. In fact it was the allegorical method that removed for Augustine the absurdity of Christianity:

> I was glad too that at last I had been shown how to interpret the ancient Scriptures of the law and the prophets in a different light from that which had previously made them seem absurd, when I used to criticize your saints for holding beliefs which they had never really held at all. . . . And when

he [Ambrose] lifted the veil of mystery and disclosed the spiritual meaning of texts which, taken literally, appeared to contain the most unlikely doctrines, I was not aggrieved by what he said, although I did not yet know whether it was true.[24]

A. M. Hunter, in reviewing the history of parable interpretation, remarks with amazement and deprecation that Augustine actually enjoyed the exercise of ingenuity involved in constructing allegorical readings and thought his audiences enjoyed it too.[25] Such a point is worth contemplation rather than dismissal. Through allegorical interpretation the ancient preacher found challenge and excitement in the Scriptures and, further, could bring them to life for his congregation. It was a way in which the "people of the Book" could continue to find inspiration and instruction in their Book, regardless of alterations in historical and cultural circumstances. The importance of allegorical interpretation to the spread of Christianity in the Greco-Roman world is hard to overemphasize. As Beryl Smalley states:

> The educated Roman convert was a rhetor rather than a philosopher. The contrast between Christianity and pagan philosophy troubled him much less than the "rustic simplicity" of the Scriptures, and their "artless" style; he missed the conventions and carefully prepared flourishes that he was accustomed to. The allegorical exposition satisfied some of his longing for complexity and ingenuity.[26]

Thus the hermeneutical concern that the early church exercised in the very construction of the gospels was discharged by the Christian community of late antiquity as well as the Middle Ages by use of the allegorical method. It gave flexibility to the relatively set writings of the church.

With the Enlightenment however came a changed sensibility in the Western world which heralded the end of allegorical exposition. The historian and the allegorist live in a different universe. The need to understand the past allegorically in order to make it fit the standards of the present was supplanted by the ability to comprehend the past as a stage in historical development that need not reflect the views of the present historical moment. The apologetic function that allegorical interpretation had once fulfilled was taken over by historical research.[27] Does historical research however fulfill the hermeneutical function of allegory? Does it help the contemporary Christian community relate the writings of the canon to the present complexities of existence? Some scholars, like Jeremias and Crossan, would probably say that historical reconstructions certainly do aid the church in hearing what the parables may mean today by elucidating what they actually meant for Jesus.[28] For others, however, the historical situation of the first century is so foreign from the problems of the twentieth that even if the actual message of Jesus could be established in all its eschatological force, a doubtful proposition, some further bridge would still be required.[29] For this latter group the historical task, though necessary and valuable, is not equivalent to the hermeneutical task. The eschatological emphasis, which the early church itself needed to moderate and mediate in the production of the gospels, requires even greater moderation and mediation to speak to the contemporary church. To reach the earliest period in the transmission of the parables, then, is not at all to interpret them to the twentieth-century community.

The problem of canonization remains a potent one. How do ancient and culturally alien texts, decreed to be perennially authoritative, continue to speak to the changing situations present through the centuries of church life?[30] If we can no longer find solace in allegorization and if for many of us historical reconstructions either are disappointing or at best still leave part of the job undone, perhaps one answer may lie in a perception of the flexibility and ambiguity basic to some of the literary forms within the canon itself. Though the parables have maintained a fairly restricted written tradition in the canonical gospels through the centuries, they have also participated in a vital oral tradition of preaching and teaching that has without qualm or hesitation removed them from their gospel settings and placed them in close relation to the problems and concerns of each period from the church fathers to the present.[31] In the light of this "oral" tradition of parable interpretation and in the light of the hermeneutical dilemma of the contemporary Christian community, the attempt to develop literary-critical tools and techniques to help open the parables to modern issues and concerns seems amply justified. A literary approach to the parables which is concerned not with what they may have meant either to Jesus or to the early church but with what they might mean now in relation to the complex theories and issues of the twentieth century is not designed to supplant historical criticism but rather to provide an additional option for modern scholarship to explore.

By learning to exploit the polyvalency of the parable form, then, we may tap at least one source of flexibility and vitality within the canon itself. The polyvalency of the parables is not something we need to fear or protect ourselves against; it is rather an opportunity for preachers, teachers, and scholars alike to discover the ways in which ancient scriptural material can interact with contemporary cultural concerns.

Yet in this discovery we must exercise care. Although flexibility is fine, unlimited interpretations constitute anarchy. Hence some guidelines for interpretation should be set up, and evaluative criteria need to be explored.

To interpret the parables within modern contexts as diverse as, for example, Jungian psychology, structuralism, and existentialism, the interpreter requires at least a glimpse of a road map. The beginnings of just such a map form the purpose of the next chapter.

CHAPTER IV

Guidelines
for Interpretation

"How then will you understand all the parables?" (Mark 4:13b). With these words the Markan Jesus gently chides his disciples for their questions about the parables before expounding to them an allegorical reading of the parable of the Sower. So too could the words probe a study such as this. To explore theoretical questions concerning the nature of the parable form is important and necessary, but without a discussion of the practical "how" of parable interpretation the theoretical study is incomplete. *How* are we to understand the parables? *How* are we to exploit the polyvalency of the parable form with restraint and sensitivity? The purpose of this chapter is to propose some guidelines for interpretation, in fact to suggest a map of some of the points which ought to be considered in a literary approach to the parables. Before beginning the map, however, we need to get our theoretical bearings by reviewing briefly what we have already discovered concerning the parables.

The examination of a semiotic and a rhetorical model for the parable form disclosed in the first place that the parables demand interpretation. In terms of the semiotic model, the indeterminate parable text requires that the interpreter supply the second-order signified in order to complete the signification process at work within the story. Similarly the rhetorical model reveals the absence of a tenor in the epiphoric-type movement of the parable, an absence which must be remedied in order for the story to function metaphorically. Hence interpretation is not a choice for one who wishes to understand the parables; it is a requirement. The parables compel the active involvement of the interpreter whether or not she or he is self-consciously aware of that involvement. Many scholars have recognized that the parables demand from their perceivers a response to the world view manifest in them.[1] What these scholars failed to see however was that the parables oblige their hearers not only to respond to the world view of the story but actually to participate in creating that world view.[2] This participation entails at least two elements: the choice of a context within which the parables may be read, and the formation of the intent of the entire interpretive process, based on the particular interests, insights, values, and concerns of the individual interpreter.

The rhetorical model in particular stresses the influence of the specific context within which a parable is viewed on the final interpretation of it. The diaphoric-type movement within the parable story functions to combine that story with its immediate surrounding images, ideas, or notions. The meaning of the parable as a whole is, then, partially composed of a synthesis between the story and its specific context. Thus different contexts necessarily result in different interpretations. As we saw in Chapter III, the interpreter may choose to use the contexts supplied by the gospel narratives. For various reasons, however, these gospel settings often prove to be problematic, and many interpreters, either because they are concerned to reconstruct the original message of Jesus or because they wish to open the parables to modern issues or both, have chosen to remove the parables from the gospels and place them in other contexts (e. g., the eschatology of Jesus, existentialism, Jungian psychology, structuralism). The first hearers of Jesus' parables may not have had this freedom to choose the context within which to view them, but they were the only group who has not. From the pregospel traditions of the early church, through the gospels themselves, through the allegorical systems of the Middle Ages, to the hermeneutical concerns of the modern period, interpreters have consistently had some freedom in selecting the particular surroundings within which to interpret individual parables.

In Chapter III, after discussing the difficulties apparent in some of the gospel presentations of the parables, we were able to formulate several practical guidelines for choosing appropriate contexts, based on the assumption that a context should not violate the parable story in any way. Thus the context must relate to the elements of the story; it should preserve a consistent focus both within itself and on the parable story; and it should fit the entire configuration of the story, not just one section of it. With further reflection these guidelines could probably be expanded, but they are sufficient to give some direction to the interpreter, who is participating in the creation of the parable world by selecting its context.

INTERPRETATION AS ART

Whether the interpreter chooses to provide a context for the parables or decides to use the contexts supplied by the gospel tradition, he or she participates in the creation of the world of the parable in another, more personal way. In describing the external source for the material used to determine what particular second-order signified will complete the signification process of a parable, Susan Wittig states:

> The second-order signified is supplied by the perceiver out of a rule-governed dynamic system of beliefs and conventions and experiences through which he finds significance in the world. . . .
> It is likely that the signified owes as much to the meaning system in the mind of the perceiver as it does to the signifier itself.[3]

The particular insights, understandings, and values of the interpreter become part of the interpretive process. The rhetorical model, furthermore, reinforces this personal participation of the interpreter by disclosing the reader's role in formulating a tenor to complete the epiphoric-type movement of the story. Hence in many cases the reader or interpreter can actually provide the intention and concerns which form the interpretation, though such a reading may be a very personal and idiosyncratic one. Yet even when the material used to determine the nature of the tenor or the second-order signified is controlled primarily by traditional doctrines or the pervasive influence of a specific context, the personal sensitivity, interest, and perspective of the interpreter supply a *focus* through which this traditional or contextual material acts upon the parable story.[4] As we saw in Chapter I, two existential interpretations of a parable or two historical interpretations of it can diverge radically from each other, depending upon the particular *focus* provided by the individual interpreter.

Thus the interpreter chooses not only the specific context, be it traditional or not, but also the particular focus or orientation that guides the entire process. The actual tenor or second-order signified that is articulated at the completion of interpretation is derived from the subtle and complex interrelationships and interdependencies among these three: the parable story, the context, and the particular insights, sensitivity, and concerns of the interpreter. When we speak of the choice of context and the particular focus resulting from the interpreter's personal concerns as separate elements, we are necessarily simplifying and categorizing what in reality are inextricably interwoven facets. The choice of the context is heavily influenced by the concerns of the interpreter, just as the context in its turn can alter, modify, or confirm those special interests. Hence in interpreting a parable three elements interact: the parable story itself, the context within which the story is viewed, and the insight, sensitivity, understanding, and concerns of the individual interpreter. An interpretation of a parable therefore not only seeks to understand the world view of the story but it also actually participates in the creation of that world view. For the parables the interpreter is in fact the cocreator.

The parables invite, even compel the interpreter to become a creator, to engage the text by joining in the creation of its meaning. In so doing he or she not only opens the parable story to current issues and problems but also opens himself or herself to the process of understanding the story. The context and the focus chosen by the interpreter spring from the personal system of meaning embraced by that particular human being. Thus the process of interpreting the parables can reveal much about the values, concerns, and priorities of the individual. Each new interpretation is a new revelation not only of the possible meanings available within the parable story itself but also of the personal world of values and meanings residing in the interpreter. It is not as the new hermeneuts would have it that the parable story alone interprets the interpreter; it is rather that in the *process* of interpretation the interpreter reveals his or her own world of meaning. As Wittig has said: "If the parable has any single, dependable meaning, it is that the human mind creates significance, and can understand itself completely only when it can comprehend itself in the act of making meaning."[5]

If the parable interpreter is in fact a creator, then parable interpretation, like all interpretation, is an art rather than a learned skill or technology. The understanding of the individual that induces him or her to interact lightly, sensitively, and perceptively with the stories is ultimately a matter of intuitive grasp rather than practiced methodology. Such a statement does not demean the methodology, however, for the most talented painters or novelists cannot succeed without practicing and mastering the techniques essential to their art. Just so, though one affirms that parable interpretation is ultimately a creative art, one also asserts the necessity of learning and mastering the techniques of literary and historical criticism essential to such an interpretive process. The remainder of this chapter will be devoted to a brief study of what some of those techniques might be. Since throughout this study the emphasis has been upon a literary approach to the parables, it is to aspects of literary criticism that our attention will be directed. Historical criticism, however, in its exploration of the general milieu and setting of texts, forms the indispensable foundation for any literary investigation of ancient or culturally alien works. The critical insights available from historical criticism of the New Testament are assumed in our study.[6]

TWO AXIOMS

In the preceding discussion we have emphasized the interpreter's participation in the creation of the parable world. For the rest of this chapter we will stress the third element in the interpretive process, the parable story itself. Though it is "we who bring the text to life,"[7] the existence of the text itself establishes the necessary precondition for the entire interpretive process. If we are to avoid anarchy in the proliferation of interpretations while yet exploiting the polyvalency of the parable form, the parable story itself must remain the controlling element in the interpretive process. It is the given with which the interpreter must work, and if the preservation of its integrity as a story is the guiding principle of interpretation, the text itself can provide limitations and restraints within which the interpreter, then, will be able to exercise her or his creative activity. Thus the first major axiom of this study is that *preservation of the integrity of the parable story should be the guiding principle of all interpretations.* Just as in Chapter III any specific context was deemed inappropriate that violated the logic or movement of the story, so any interpretation which violates the parable story must also be judged inappropriate. This criterion draws force from the disclosure by the semiotic model of the need for congruency between the second-order signifier, the story, and the second-order signified, the interpretation.

Hence the interpretation must "fit" the parable story. Further, it must deal with the entire configuration of the story and not just one part of it, although not all parts may be of equal importance. For example interpretations of the parable of the Prodigal Son that discuss only the actions of the prodigal and omit the episode concerning the elder son are inappropriate readings of that parable. Moreover the final interpretation should be consistent within itself, and if some contemporary system is chosen as the context or as part of the general focus of the interpretation, that system should be subject to evaluation on its own merits as well as on its success in "fitting" the story. If one formulated a reading of a parable from the perspective of Nazi ideology, for instance, it could be criticized not only from the standpoint of its appropriateness to the particular parable story, but also on the basis of the cogency of Nazi ideology itself.

If the preservation of the integrity of the parable story is to be the guiding principle for interpretation, the question that quite naturally arises is how the total configuration of that story may be known so that it can fulfill this function. A full exploration and understanding of the individual parable story itself becomes the necessary first step in interpretation. Axiomatic to such an exploration is the assertion that *in a literary work form and content, though distinguishable, are inseparable;*[8] therefore a proper articulation of the meanings of a particular text is inextricably bound to a proper understanding of its special form.[9] Hence parable interpretation begins in the literary-critical task of discerning the formal patterns and structures which compose the surface narratives of the individual stories. In the sections which follow we will investigate some literary-critical tools for exploring the parables in light of this second axiom, the inseparability of form and content.

THE PARABLE TEXT

Before investigating the formal patterns or surface narrative structures of a particular parable one must first resolve a preliminary issue: which textual version of a parable is to be used? We are assuming at this point that a fairly stable manuscript tradition underlies the Greek text of most of the parables. That being so, among the parables that appear in only one gospel setting, two options occur: one can choose to study the parable text as it appears in the gospel, or using established criteria one may attempt to construct a hypothetical text closer in form to the postulated *Ur*-parable spoken by Jesus. For those parables having more than one gospel setting the options are three: one may arbitrarily select one gospel version to explore, or one may choose a gospel version based upon a predetermined criterion, or again, one may try to reconstruct a hypothetical text.

The use of hypothetical texts is certainly warranted if the ultimate goal is to elicit information concerning the historical Jesus. The difficulties involved in establishing hypothetical texts and in using them, difficulties which we have already mentioned, are such however that their use is not to be encouraged in any case other than one involving a reconstruction of the message of the historical Jesus.[10] For a study which for whatever reasons aims at being primarily literary, an extant gospel version of the parable is preferable. Even when one is not planning to employ the gospel context, the extant parable story found within that gospel context can be removed and studied on its own. A literary study attempting to explore the structural patterns of the surface narrative is on firmer ground with a real, extant text than with a hypothetical one in which the structural patterns may have been disrupted. In investigating a gospel version of a parable, whether using the gospel context or not, the literary critic is in fact exploring the *final form* of the parable.

Employing the final form of the parable is clear enough for those that appear in only one gospel setting, but what is the literary critic to do when faced with parables that have two or three separate gospel versions? With parables in a double or triple tradition the interpreter may simply choose one version arbitrarily or, perhaps the better option, choose a version on the basis of some literary criterion, such as the fullest narrative, the most carefully patterned narrative, the most complete or most economically rendered story. The latter possibility, though not involving an arbitrary decision, also does not provide a basis for asserting that the chosen final form is better, older, or more authentic than the other final forms of the parable. Such evaluative assessments of one version over another must be argued on grounds other than the ones suggested above. Having selected a parable text to study, however, the interpreter qua literary critic must now begin to explore the formal patterns composing the surface narrative of that story.

NARRATIVE STRUCTURE

The interpreter's primary concern is to arrive at a reading of one particular parable story; it is not a concern with the sociological, cultural, or mythological potentials of parables in general, though those are certainly legitimate interests. For an interpreter however whose goal is to comprehend one parable in terms of one particular issue, the emphasis must fall on the dramatic development of its special story, differing in many ways from each of the other parable stories. It is not what the parables as a group may share but what makes each one a distinctive narrative that engages the effort of the interpreter. To use Paul Ricoeur's terminology, it is the narrative message rather than the underlying code that is of value to the hermeneut.[11] Hence the narrative structure that needs to be studied by the interpreter is the *surface structure* of the story, for this surface structure embodies the message of the parable.[12] Structuralism, based as it is on a linguistic model, has not proved helpful in this type of study because its major aim is "to determine the nature of the system underlying the event"[13] rather than the nature of the particular event itself. In fact Ricoeur has said:

> Structuralism, to my mind, is a dead end the very moment when it treats any "message" as the mere "quotation" of its underlying "code." This claim alone makes structural method structuralist prejudice. Structuralism as ideology starts with the reversal in the relation between code and message which makes the code essential and the message unessential. And it is because this step is taken that the text is killed as message *and* that no existential interpretation seems appropriate for a message which has been reduced to a pure epiphenomenon of the "codes."[14]

Thus since our concern is with the message level of particular stories, the structural analysis we need to develop is the analysis of surface patterns and forms. It is the *surface structure* of the parables, not the deep structure, which this study intends to analyze, for to explore the surface structure is to begin investigating what messages a particular story may bear.[15]

The analysis of the surface patterns and structures of parable stories can be accomplished through a number of approaches. It is our purpose to discuss only two of those: the analysis of the manner of discourse and the exploration of rhetorical style. These approaches are meant to be illustrative, rather than exhaustive, of the kinds of analyses that discover the patterns and structures composing the parables' surface narratives. Our intent is to explore as fully as possible the total configuration of the parable story, both as a guide to interpretation and as a limiting check on interpretation, for as we noted above, if the interpretation violates the integrity of the story, it is inappropriate. These investigations of the surface structures and patterns of the parables attempt to clarify further what elements constitute such a total configuration.

The Manner of Discourse

One of the earliest and most discerning of all discussions of literary art is found in Aristotle's *Poetics*. For Aristotle the central element in all art, or imitation, as he expressed it, is the *object* of imitation, and this object consists of agents involved in actions. Thus one preliminary aspect of exploring the surface patterns of the parables is to determine what actions and how many actions are involved in the plot of the story. For example the parable of the Lost Coin (Luke 15:8–9) involves one agent completing one action, though the action has three parts: losing, finding, rejoicing. The parable of the Pharisee and the Publican (Luke 18:10–14) concerns two agents involved in two separate actions. Among the parables that involve two actions there appear to be two major formal types of a very general nature: a concentric circle type and a parallel plot type. The concentric circle parables, like the Wicked Tenants, the Unjust Steward, and the Unmerciful Servant, all involve one action encircled by another. The first action begins (e.g., the master forgives the servant); then the second action begins and ends (e.g., the servant is begged by another servant for forgiveness, refuses, and has the second servant jailed); finally, the initial action is completed (e.g., the master recalls the servant and throws him in jail). The parallel plot type appears in parables like the Prodigal Son, the Workers in the Vineyard, the Pharisee and the Publican, and the Two Sons. In these parables one action begins and ends (e.g., the younger son leaves home and returns) and then the second action begins and ends (e.g., the elder son returns home and argues with the father). In most of the double action parables of both types there is usually one character who is involved in both sections and who therefore tends to add continuity to the full story.

Once this preliminary evaluation of the plot is accomplished, an analysis of the manner of discourse within the story can begin. Aristotle identifies three manners of imitation: the narrative mode, the dramatic mode, and the mixed mode. In essence he is examining narrated discourse, direct discourse, or some combination of the two. Most stories, naturally, fall into the category of the mixed mode; that is, they contain both narrated discourse and direct discourse. What is valuable in this distinction is that the decision of which mode to use at what moment is basically a matter of the storyteller's discretion. As Aristotle says:

> For, using the same means and imitating the same kinds of object, it is possible for the poet on different occasions to narrate the story (either speaking in the person of one of his characters as Homer does or in his own person without changing roles) or to have the imitators performing and acting out the entire story.[16]

The creator of the story, then, has a great deal of freedom in the choice of what manner of discourse to use at any moment. A change in the manner of discourse can function as a structural signal to the perceivers of the story that some kind of distinction is being made.

The most obvious observation to be made about the difference between narrated discourse and direct discourse is the presence of narrative distance. Whenever the narrator relates an event rather than having a character speak directly, an element of distance has been added to the story. This element of distance has many uses: It may serve to highlight some parts of the story by playing down others. For instance in the parable of the Prodigal Son (Luke 15:11–32) most of the exploits of the younger son in the far country are narrated. Direct discourse is employed only at the crucial moment when the prodigal comes to himself and decides to return to his father. Shifting the manner of discourse, then, may serve to emphasize one aspect of the story by heightening its dramatic effect in relation to the surrounding material. Narrative distance may also be used to tone down elements of the story that might prove distracting to the perceiver. In the parable of the Wicked Tenants (Matt. 21:33–41/Mark 12:1–9/Luke 20:9–16), for example, the killing of the son is related in narrated discourse rather than in a direct discourse pronouncement by one of the characters, such as "I have him, and I'm sticking my knife into his ribs," or something similar, which would in fact be a distracting note in the movement of the story.

By allowing the shifts in the manner of discourse to mark off sections of the stories, the interpreter can begin to see some surface structural patterns take shape. These patterns, then, guide the interpreter in noting the emphases and nuances of the plot. To illustrate the use of an analysis of the manner of discourse let us look at two parables of the parallel plot type, the Two Sons (Matt. 21:28–31a) and the Pharisee and the Publican (Luke

18:10–14a). By its basic formulation the parallel plot type encourages an immediate comparison of the two sections of the parable. Often this comparison is sharpened into an overt opposition. Further, this type can allow for relatively greater complexity than is generally found in parables because it in effect tells two separate stories, either or both of which can contain the concentric circle pattern (so the first section of both the Prodigal Son and the Workers in the Vineyard). The parables of the Two Sons and the Pharisee and the Publican however are not of such complexity, though they clearly display the oppositional character of the parallel plot type. They are moreover remarkably similar in structure, and we will list them side by side for greater ease of comparison (ND will stand for narrated discourse and DD for direct discourse). In general it is probably permissible to count such stage directions as "he went to him and said," followed by a direct quotation, as part of the direct discourse unit; however, for the purpose of illustration we will occasionally be more stringent than necessary in what follows.

TWO SONS (Matt. 21:28–31a)	PHARISEE AND PUBLICAN (Luke 18:10–14a)
Introduction	
A ND: A man had two sons;	ND: Two men went up to the temple to pray, one a Pharisee and the other a tax collector.
First Action	
B DD: and he went to the first and said, "Son, go and work in the vineyard today." And he answered, "I will not";	DD: The Pharisee stood and prayed thus with himself, "God, I thank thee that I am not like other men, extortioners, unjust, adulterers, or even like this tax collector. I fast twice a week, I give tithes of all that I get."
Shift	
C ND: but afterward he repented and went. And he went to the second and said the same;	ND: But the tax collector, standing far off, would not even lift up his eyes to heaven, but beat his breast,
Second Action	
B′ DD: and he answered, "I go, sir,"	DD: saying, "God, be merciful to me a sinner!"

Conclusion

| A' ND: but did not go. Which of the two did the will of his father? | ND: I tell you, this man went down to his house justified rather than the other. |

The two opposing actions of both parables are carefully interwoven with each other: they begin with a narrated introduction which presents the characters (A); next, the first action is set in direct discourse as is the second action (B–B'); both parables shift from one action to the other by means of a section of narrated discourse (C); and finally, they end with a narrated evaluative conclusion addressed to the audience (A'), albeit a different type of narration from that found in A and C. In both parables the direct discourse of the first action is longer than that of the second. The careful interlocking of the opposing sections suggests a certain unity in opposition: One encounter is incomplete without its opposite, formally speaking. The Pharisee cannot exist without the publican and vice versa, just as the son who says no and goes cannot exist without the son who says yes and does not go. This formal unification of opposites opens these stories to, among other things, possible existential speculations concerning the nature of opposition itself.

Clearly the similarities between these two parables are great. Yet in terms of content they apparently stress and approve the actions of opposite characters. In the Two Sons the first son does 'the will of the father, while in the Pharisee and the Publican the second, the publican, is approved and commended. Rudolf Bultmann, in fact, following the folkloric law of end stress, suggests that the order of the Two Sons should be reversed, so that the section concerning the son who says no but eventually goes comes last in the story.[17] However, the formal patterning of these parables confirms the evaluation of the content. Both stories are structured in parallel units of narrated and direct discourse that swing around a narrated center section. That center section discloses the key to the opposing character evaluations of the two parables. In the parable of the Pharisee and the Publican the center section is totally concerned with the publican; it points exclusively in his direction. On the other hand the center section of the Two Sons contains the important reference to the ultimate obedience of the first son; it points clearly toward him. Hence these shift passages are central not only in terms of the formal structure of the surface narratives but also in terms of an evaluation of the content of the parables. They disclose the directions stressed by the entire configuration of the plots.

Some of the ways in which an analysis of the manner of discourse increases the interpreter's understanding of the plot structure of the parables can be seen from this brief example. Such an analysis may be used alone, or it may be combined with other methods in order to explore in greater detail the internal relations of a text. It is particularly suited for providing clues to the points of stress or emphasis within a story. We will return to this method again in combination with another, but for the moment let us move on to a brief discussion of rhetorical style.

The Rhetorical Style

Just as literary style itself can be defined in a number of ways, analyses of style display a wide diversity of approaches and assumptions.[18] Our particular approach to style will take its lead from rhetorical criticism as developed for the Hebrew Scriptures by James Muilenburg.[19] According to Muilenburg one of the major concerns of the rhetorical critic is "to note the various rhetorical devices that are employed for marking, on the one hand, the sequence and movement of the pericope, and on the other, the shifts and breaks" in its evolution.[20] Most important among these rhetorical devices is the repetition of words and phrases in parallel or chiastic designs:

> [Repetition] served as an effective mnemonic device. It is the key word which may often guide us in our isolation of a literary unit, which gives to it its unity and focus, which helps us to articulate the structure of the composition, and to discern the pattern or texture into which the words are woven. It is noteworthy that repetitions are most abundant in crucial contexts.[21]

Repetitions of words and phrases, besides being most prevalent in the crucial segments of the story, tend to form discernible patterns. The parallel pattern of repetition is one in which one or more words or phrases are repeated in the same order. For instance in Mark 4:33–34[22] the openings of each verse create parallel repetitions:

33: And with many such <u>parables,</u>^a <u>he spoke to them</u>^b
    the word, as they were able to hear it;
34: but without a <u>parable</u>^{a′} <u>he spoke to them</u>^{b′}
    not, but privately to his disciples he explained everything.

Repetitions can also involve word variations, as do these parallel lines in Mark 4:21:

Is a <u>lamp</u>^a (*ho lychnos*) brought in <u>to be put</u>^b (*tethẹ̄*)
    under a bushel or under a bed?
(Is it) not on a <u>lampstand</u>^{a′} (*lychnian*) <u>to be put</u>^{b′} (*tethẹ̄*)?

Forming a pattern of a, b, a', b', parallel repetitions hold a unit together and encourage a comparison between its segments.

The chiastic pattern of repetition, on the other hand, describes words or phrases that are subsequently repeated in an *inverted* order within a unit.[23] One of the clearest and most familiar of the chiastic repetitions in the New Testament is found in Mark 2:27:

<blockquote>
       a   b   b'   a'
The <u>sabbath</u> for <u>man</u> was made and not the <u>man</u> for the <u>sabbath</u>.
</blockquote>

As can be seen, chiastic repetitions usually form a pattern of a, b, b', a'. Chiasmus moreover may be present in inverted orders other than those of repeated words; for instance the grammatical structure object-verb-verb-object also forms a chiasmus.[24] A fully developed chiastic design often contains a center element, a word, phrase, or even sentence that the inverted order swings around. The pattern then becomes a, b, c, b', a'. Chiastic repetitions containing this central aspect tend to focus attention inward toward it. In fact all chiastic repetitions, whether or not they contain one center element, as compared to parallel repetitions, tend to provide a more tightly knit structure to their units. A visual and spatial metaphor might be of assistance in elucidating this point. Chiasmus is named after the Greek letter chi which is formed by placing two bars crosswise: X. Chiastic repetition within a unit duplicates this design:

The pattern therefore can be described spatially as centering at one internal point and expanding outward in diagonal directions. Or if one reverses the movement, it can be described as beginning at four diverse points and focusing into the center. Parallel repetition patterns, on the other hand, do not evince this inward (or outward) movement; rather, like parallel lines they move along in the same direction but never meet. They do not focus toward the center or out from the center but along the horizontal. Like parallel lines these repetition patterns establish clear internal relationships, but there is always some distance between them.

As an example of an analysis of rhetorical style let us look at two parables from the fourth chapter of Mark, the parable of the Seed Growing Secretly (vv. 26–29) and the parable of the Mustard Seed (vv. 30–32). Both parables use the narrated manner of discourse exclusively. They both begin with references to the kingdom of God (vv. 26 and 30) and they both end with allusions to the Hebrew Scriptures (v. 29b alludes to Joel 3:13 and

v. 32c alludes to Ezek. 17:23, 31:6, and Dan. 4:21). Finally, they both are
concerned with seeds and growth. Hence in terms of their content these
two parables display many similarities. Formally, the central sections of
both parables contain repetition patterns:

<table>
<tr><td align="center">SEED GROWING SECRETLY
(Mark 4:26–29)</td><td align="center">MUSTARD SEED
(Mark 4:30–32)</td></tr>
</table>

Introduction

And he said, "The kingdom of God is	And he said, "With what can we compare the kingdom of God, or what parable shall we use for it?

Central Section

as if (*hōs*) a man should scatter seed^a (*sporon*) on the earth^b (*gēs*) and should sleep and rise night and day, and the seed^{a′} (*sporon*) should sprout and grow, he knows not how. The earth^{b′} (*gē*) produces of itself, first the blade, then the ear, then the full grain in the ear. But when the crop permits, at once	Like (*hōs*) a grain of mustard seed, which, when it is sown^a (*hotan sparē*) on the earth^b (*epi tēs gēs*), is the smallest of all the seeds^c on the earth^{b′} (*epi tēs gēs*), yet when it is sown^{a′} (*hotan sparē*), it grows up and becomes the greatest of all shrubs, and puts forth large branches, so that

Allusion to Hebrew Scripture

he puts in the sickle, because the harvest has come." (Cf. Joel 3:13.)	the birds of the air can make nests in its shade." (Cf. Ezek. 17:23, 31:6, and Dan. 4:21.)

The repetitions in both parables involve the words (or in the case of the
Mustard Seed, phrases) for seed or sowing and the earth. Moreover the
repetitions occur in the crucial central section of the parables. The parable
of the Seed Growing Secretly contains a pattern of parallel repetition, while
the Mustard Seed evinces a chiastic one. The different patterns displayed
by these two parables once again confirm the inseparability of form and
content. The parallel repetitions in the surface structure of the Seed Growing Secretly reinforce and underline the concurrent descriptions of the man,
scattering the seed, sleeping and rising, and of the seed, sprouting in the
earth, growing to harvest, even though the parallel words themselves refer

exclusively to elements of the plant world. The content tells the story of the related but separate actions of the man and the seed while a formal patterning of parallel repetition highlights that content in a slightly skewed fashion. The correspondence between the form and the content of the parable of the Mustard Seed however is remarkably exact. The a, b, c, b', a' pattern focuses attention in upon "the smallest of all the seeds." That tiny seed forms the central point of the chiastic structure. And just as the seed when sown on the earth grows to the greatest of all shrubs, so the chiasmus spreads out from that central point to encompass the entire unit in its structural design. Thus the development of the small seed into the great shrub coincides with the inward and outward movement of the chiastic repetition pattern, while the concurrence of the course of human life with the growth of plant life finds confirmation in a pattern of parallel repetition. The surface structures of both of these parables, analyzed on the basis of rhetorical style, disclose and exemplify the movements, emphases, and directions of each story as a whole.

In this brief example of rhetorical criticism and in the discussion preceding it, we have noted only patterns of repetition consisting of four (or five) elements. Both parallel and chiastic repetitions can contain still more words and phrases. For example the parable of the Unjust Judge (Luke 18:2–5) contains a pattern of parallel repetition that involves six elements, three in the first half and three in the second half:

THE UNJUST JUDGE
(Luke 18:2–5)

In a certain city there was a judge who <u>neither</u>[a] <u>feared God nor regarded man</u>[b]; and there was a <u>widow</u> in that city who kept coming to him and saying, "<u>Vindicate</u>[c] me against my adversary."

For a while he refused; but afterward he said to himself, "Though I <u>neither fear God nor regard man</u>[a'], yet because this <u>widow</u>[b'] bothers me, I will <u>vindicate</u>[c'] her or she will wear me out by her continual coming."

In this parable the repetition pattern is a, b, c, a', b', c'. Hence it is quite possible for repetitions in the parables to involve more than four words or phrases, though the larger the number, the less often the pattern appears.

Throughout our discussion of repetition we have judged as legitimate examples only those units containing repetitions of precise words or phrases, or variations thereof.[25] If the exact word or word-variation is not iterated, then the repetition pattern is not present. The conservative formulation of this principle is an attempt to guard against the abuses of this type of analysis which turn it into a theme or motif study. The difficulty presented by an analysis that relies upon the repetition of a theme to indicate structural patterns is that without using exact word repetition as an anchor a motif or theme may be construed in any of a variety of ways in order to make it fit a particular schema.

Kenneth Bailey in his book *Poet and Peasant* is often guilty of substituting theme repetition for exact word repetition in order to manipulate the material into one of his literary types. For instance in analyzing Acts 4:8–12 he uses parallel themes to demonstrate the parallelism between two stanzas. The first stanza begins, "Rulers of the people and elders of Israel" (v. 8), in which Bailey finds the theme "you rulers." This first theme is supposedly paralleled by the beginning of the second stanza, "by the name of Jesus Christ of Nazareth, whom you crucified, whom God raised from the dead" (v. 10), in which the matching theme is "you crucified." Surely even the assertion that these themes are parallel strains one's credulity, without raising the question of how he arrived at these particular themes in the first place. Furthermore Bailey finds in the second line of stanza one, "if we are being examined today concerning a good deed to a cripple" (v. 9), the theme of "a man whole." Though the theme "a man whole" might not occur to everyone reading that line, it does occur to Bailey, primarily, one suspects, because the second line of stanza two mentions "a man whole."[26] Bailey's parallel themes often become as universal and general as "Do," "Go," or "Act."[27] Clearly any literary text can be made to fit any theme pattern if the themes are sufficiently general and the interpreter sufficiently imaginative. The "parabolic ballad" pattern that Bailey unearths for most of the parables in Luke is based almost exclusively on this kind of motif analysis.[28] Such a method however is so idiosyncratic that it is practically useless to other interpreters. Hence to insure the viability of the method it is necessary to insist upon the presence of exact word, word-variation, or phrase repetition in analyzing the parallel or chiastic patterns within the surface narrative of a text.

We have investigated in this section two methods for clarifying the surface structure of the parables: an analysis of the manner of discourse and an explication of rhetorical style. In most of the examples we have studied for both methods we have found it enlightening to compare similarly structured parables together. Such comparisons have highlighted the differences and similarities in the structure of each individual parable. In fact this practice of clustering parables together on the basis of corresponding patterns or structures can provide much useful information for the interpreter. It is another guideline for interpretation.

CLUSTERING THE PARABLES

In Chapter III we discussed the notion that supplying a context was in fact a way of lengthening the narrative of the parable to include that specific context. This kind of lengthening is necessary because of the sheer brevity of most parable stories themselves; they are too short for the effective use of many literary-critical tools. In the last section of this chapter we noted in practice the usefulness of grouping parables together to explore with greater clarity the patterns within each one. In effect, grouping or clustering parables together in this way extends the length of the narrative of each, just as providing some other context would do, and thus gives the interpreter more material upon which to draw in understanding the total configuration of the plots.

This idea of clustering the parables together to aid interpretation is not new. John Dominic Crossan, for example, suggested grouping together the nine parables that share the master-servant theme.[29] This cluster of Servant parables however is delineated primarily by the thematic unity of the parables rather than by similarities in their structure, though Crossan does attempt to find common structural patterns within the group.[30] We are suggesting the clustering of parables primarily by means of their surface structural similarities rather than by reference to their themes or motifs. Clustering parables together does provide each parable with a kind of context which will influence its final interpretation. Moreover comparing a parable with a number of similarly structured ones will probably in each case highlight or stress different elements of the parable's surface structure and therefore imply different alternatives for the interpretive process.

As an illustration of this practice of clustering the parables together, as well as an illustration of the usefulness of combining both the methods of structural analysis we have just investigated, let us explore the parable of the Unjust Steward (Luke 16:1–8a) read against the background of the parable of the Wicked Tenants (Mark 12:1–9/Matt. 21:33–41/Luke 20:9–16/Gospel of Thomas 93:1–16). Both parables involve double actions and fall into the general category we have called the concentric circle type. Generally this type consists of a pattern in which one action is started (Ia), then a second action is started and finished (IIa–d), and finally, the first action is completed (Ib). Further, both parables contain chiastic and parallel repetition patterns in their crucial segments (for the Wicked Tenants, section IIa, and for the Unjust Steward, mainly section IId). The parable of the Unjust Steward has long been a problem for interpreters. Various solutions have been offered, including seeing the parable as irony,[31] as an example of almsgiving,[32] or as a depiction of the picaresque mode.[33] Battles have also raged for both parables over where the stories should end. Since both parables are considered examples of the concentric circle type, with an initial agent involved in an action (in both a master), a second action involving other agents (here servants), and a final action involving the initial agent once again, both Luke 16:8a and Mark 12:9[34] are essential to the logic and movement of the narratives.[35] Without these endings both narratives are truncated; they do not end, they merely stop.

Analyzing the parables side by side on the basis of manner of discourse (direct discourse is DD and narrated discourse ND), chiastic and parallel repetitions of words and phrases, and a very careful reading, one finds six basic divisions within both parables:

Ia. Introduction of the initial agent, the master, and setting of the scene (ND)

IIa. Wrongdoing of secondary agents, the servants (ND)

IIb. Decision of the master (mainly DD)

IIc. Evaluation of situation by the servants (DD)

IId. Action of the servants (ND for the Tenants and DD for the Steward)

Ib. Resolving action of the master (ND)

The texts of the parables, separated into these divisions and written in parallel columns, would look like this:

PARABLE OF
THE WICKED TENANTS
(Mark 12:1–9)

PARABLE OF
THE UNJUST STEWARD
(Luke 16:1–8)

Ia. Narrated Setting of Scene (ND)

12:1 And he began to speak to them in parables. "A man **planted a vineyard, and set a hedge around it, and dug a pit for the wine press, and built a tower,** and let it out to tenants, and went into another country.

16:1a,b He also said to the disciples, "There was a rich man who had a steward,

IIa.   Narrated Wrongdoing of Servant(s) (ND)

12:2–5 And he sent (*kai apesteilen*)
to the tenants at that time a
slave, to receive (*labē*) from
the tenants the fruit of the
vineyard; and receiving (*labontes*) him they beat him
and sent (*kai apesteilan*) him
away empty.
And again he sent (*kai palin
apesteilen*) another slave; and
they wounded him in the
head and treated him badly.
And another he sent (*kai
allon apesteilen*), and that
one they killed, and many
others, some they beat and
some they killed.

16:1c and charges were brought to
him that this man was wasting his
goods.

IIb.   Decision of Master (Mainly DD)

12:6   Still (*eti*) one other he had, a
beloved son; he sent him at
last to them, saying, 'They
will respect my son.'

16:2 And calling him he said to him,
'What is this I hear concerning you?
Turn in an account of your stewardship, for you can no longer be
steward.'

IIc.   Evaluation of Situation by Servant(s) (DD)

12:7   Those tenants, however, said
to one another, 'This is the
heir; come, let us kill him,
and the inheritance will be
ours.'

16:3–4 The steward, however, said
to himself, 'What shall I do (*ti
poiēsō*), since my master is taking
the stewardship from me? I am not
strong enough to dig, I am ashamed
to beg.
'I have decided what I shall
do (*ti poiēsō*) so that when I am put
out of the stewardship (*oikonomias*)
they will receive me into their homes
(*oikous*).'

IId. Action of Servant(s)

12:8	(ND) And seizing him, they killed him, and threw him out of the vineyard.	16:5–7 (DD) And, summoning one by one the debtors of his master, he said to the first,

(a) 'How much do you owe to my master?'
(b) He said, 'A hundred measures of oil.'
(c) And he said to him, 'Take your bill and, sitting down quickly, write fifty.'
Then he said to another,
(a') 'How much do you owe?'
(b') He said, 'A hundred measures of wheat.'
(c') He said to him, 'Take your bill and write eighty.'

Ib.   Response of Master to Action of Servant(s) (ND)

12:9	What will the master of the vineyard do? He will come and destroy the tenants, and give the vineyard to others."	16:8a And the master commended the unjust steward (*oikonomon tēs adikias*) that he did wisely (*phronimōs epoiēsen*)."

Several aspects of the analysis should be noted for both of the parables: First, the parable of the Wicked Tenants, section IIa (Mark 12:2–5) displays three carefully paralleled constructions all beginning with *kai . . . apesteilen*. Furthermore, the first of these constructions, the longest of the three, is internally structured by use of the chiastic *apesteilen . . . labē̄* . . . *labontes . . . apesteilan*. The division between IIa and IIb in the Wicked Tenants is marked not by a change in the manner of discourse, though that comes shortly, but rather by a change in the opening connective. Every sense unit in the parable up to 12:6 begins with *kai;* at 12:6 the connective pattern is altered by the use of *eti*, and such an alteration signals to the hearer or reader a difference in the narration. In the final verse of the parable the rhetorical question is answered by the narrator within the narrative itself. The use of such rhetorical questions in the parables is not particularly unusual. Bultmann has suggested that these questions may additionally indicate the relation of the parable form to the Hebrew *māšāl*.[36]

In the parable of the Unjust Steward the division between Ia and IIa is indicated by the switch from the use of verbs in imperfect indicative (*ēn* and *eichen*), describing a continuing state of existence, to verbs in the aorist (*dieblēthē* and following), which suggest grammatically the beginning of a definite historical action. Section IIc prepares for the carefully paralleled constructions of IId by a parallelism of its own, *ti poiēsō hoti* and *ti poiēsō hina*. The emphasis on *poiēsō* in this section is alluded to again in 16:8a when the servant is praised, *hoti phronimōs epoiēsen*. The master in section IIc is referred to as *ho kyrios mou*, which is picked up again in 16:8a (and also in 16:5). A play on the words *oikonomias* and *oikous* marks the end of section IIc: he who was turned out of (*ek*) his "home-tending" will be welcomed into (*eis*) their homes. Section IId, the longest division of the Unjust Steward, is composed of two carefully paralleled actions, related mostly by direct discourse. The parallelism serves to emphasize the action as does the use of direct discourse.

When read together these two parables present striking contrasts. Both parables concern masters who have unfaithful servants; yet in the Unjust Steward the servant is ultimately commended for his dishonest behavior, while in the Wicked Tenants the servants are ultimately destroyed. A comparison of their structure presents even more interesting data. The longest, most carefully designed, and crucial section of the Wicked Tenants has to do with the narrated wrongdoings of the tenants, while that section is the shortest one in the Unjust Steward. Conversely the longest sections of the Unjust Steward (IIc and d) have to do with the steward's evaluation of his situation and his ultimate action, while these are two of the shortest sections of the Wicked Tenants. Moreover the fatal action committed by the tenants is narrated and thus played down in comparison to the crucial action of the steward, which is not only given in direct discourse, and thereby highlighted by a dramatic presentation, but also presented in carefully paralleled repetitions.

Reading the Unjust Steward against the background of the Wicked Tenants serves to emphasize the steward's evaluation of his situation and his action in response to that evaluation. These are the sections of the parable with the most carefully constructed units, and these are also the sections which contrast most sharply with those of the Wicked Tenants. In the latter parable it is the wrongdoing of the tenants that is most clearly emphasized in contrast to the Unjust Steward. An interpretation of the Unjust Steward might begin at this point: There is something essential in the steward's evaluation and action that brings him commendation rather than destruction by the master. The steward, in some degree of anxiety, decides what he must do to secure a home for himself when he is thrown out of his master's. He decides that he is not strong enough to dig and could not bear to beg, and so he plans a dishonest action to secure his continued existence. He in effect decides that the preservation of his own life and happiness is of a higher priority than the honest accounting of his master's books. Society may require that certain rules be faithfully followed to keep all its cogs and wheels running, but those rules may not always be to the benefit of individual happiness and dignity.

It is at those moments of conflict between the traditional morality of society and the well-being of a particular individual when one is called upon to exercise a stewardship of injustice (cf. *ton oikonomon tēs adikias*), to make a careful evaluation of options and then, if necessary, to use the means of injustice to preserve the individual well-being. In the parable of the Wicked Tenants the tenants in a hastily made decision chose to violate the rules of society *and* the well-being of many individuals. They attempted to secure their own existence by the destruction of others and in the end were themselves destroyed. They were not good stewards of injustice; they used it to destroy human life rather than preserve it. By contrast the steward in the parable of the Unjust Steward makes a complicated decision to secure his own happiness and well-being at the expense of traditional ethics, and in so doing he displays a wise stewardship of injustice, for which he is rightly commended. The parable, on the basis of this interpretation, suggests a radical understanding of both the concept of stewardship itself and also the wise use of injustice to preserve human well-being.

A preliminary interpretation of the kind suggested above could be supplemented by the use of a more fully developed interpretive context, such as a Marxist literary criticism of the economic manipulation of the worker or a Freudian analysis of the conflict between the individual and society. The use of such an interpretive context would further lengthen the narrative and give the interpreter that much more material to analyze. However, the careful analysis of the narrative of the parable against the background of another parable of similar structure provides a strong preliminary basis for interpretation and a needed guide for further investigation.

Thus we can see from this one example how clustering parables together highlights and stresses various sections of their plots, providing a particular direction for interpretation. It is quite possible that reading the parable of the Unjust Steward against the background of some other similarly structured parable (perhaps another of the concentric circle type) would emphasize different aspects of the story and suggest a different basis for interpretation. Read against the parable of the Wicked Tenants, the commendation by the master at the end of the Unjust Steward appears to be a serious evaluation. The action of the steward to preserve his way of life is so much less destructive and less heinous than the actions of the tenants to preserve theirs that one is inclined to think he does deserve some praise for his dishonesty. Were one not reading the Unjust Steward against the background of the Wicked Tenants, but against some other context, one might well understand the master's comment at the end of the parable to be the height of irony. So clustering parables together to explore more fully their structure does indeed provide a context which may influence the final interpretation.

So far in this chapter we have been investigating guidelines for discerning information about the *form* of the parable stories. Before we conclude, we must look briefly at some elements of the *content* of the stories. Since much has already been written about plot movement and the protagonist's power of action in the parables,[37] we shall not comment further on them. But the question of the realism of the parable stories is an issue that needs some additional clarification.

✓THE PARABLES AND REALISM

One comment that is often made about the parables of Jesus, particularly in distinguishing them from Rabbinic parables or allegories, is that the stories are remarkably realistic:

> In the parables of the Gospels, however, all is true to nature and to life. Each similitude or story is a perfect picture of something that can be observed in the world of our experience. The processes of nature are accurately observed and recorded; the actions of persons in the stories are in character . . .[38]

Realism as a literary phenomenon came to full bloom during the nineteenth century in the Western world and still dominates the scene. Surely it is, then, anachronistic to speak of the presence of realism, in the modern sense, in the parables.[39] It is also misleading, for their "realism" has many gaps in it. Ricoeur has pointed to the "extravagance" of the parables, by which he means the "presence of the extraordinary within the ordinary." He thinks that this extraordinary element in the parable stories can be fully determined only by reference to other sayings of Jesus and to an interpretation of the complex symbol Kingdom of God.[40] But is it not possible to detect the "extraordinary within the ordinary" in the content of the stories themselves without having to refer to external supports? Many of the parables contain extravagant exaggerations which Joachim Jeremias attempts to explain as "characteristic of the oriental way of telling a story."[41] Characteristic or not, these exaggerated details explode the realism of the parables; yet they are part of the plot line itself and are not imposed upon the stories by an external reference.

Some of these exaggerated details are the following: the father running
out to meet his son in the Prodigal Son; the judge fearing that the widow
would beat him black and blue in the Unjust Judge; *all* of the maidens fall-
ing asleep while awaiting the bridegroom in the Ten Maidens; *all* of the
guests refusing an invitation to a feast in the Wedding Feast; the mustard
seed growing into a tree in the Mustard Seed (in Lukan and Matthean
versions);[42] the woman putting leaven into three measures of flour (which
is the equivalent of close to fifty pounds of flour, enough to feed more than
one hundred people)[43] in the Leaven; the servant owing his master ten
thousand talents in the Unmerciful Servant (the magnitude of the sum can
be appreciated when one realizes that the entire tribute paid to Rome by
Galilee and Peraea in 4 B.C. amounted to two hundred talents, one fiftieth of
that debt).[44] All of these elements within the stories themselves evidence
the presence of the "extraordinary within the ordinary," the clearly symbolic
within the realistic.

Robert Scholes and Robert Kellogg in their excellent study *The Nature of
Narrative* propose that the relation between the worlds of fiction and the
world of reality can be either representational or illustrative:

> The images of a narrative may strike us at once as an attempt to create a
> replica of actuality . . . or they may strike us as an attempt merely to
> remind us of an aspect of reality rather than convey a total and convincing
> impression of the real world to us. . . . The illustrative is symbolic; the
> representational is mimetic.[45]

On the basis of this schematization the parables would certainly be more
illustrative than representational, for they do not really "create a replica of
actuality." As we noted in Chapter III the very brevity and economy of the
stories prevents them from fully developing characters or plots. Parable
characters, in fact, are more "types," or in Aristotelian terms "agents," than
they are humanized individuals with emotions and inner drives. As Scholes
and Kellogg put it:

> In every case, whenever we consider a character as a type, we are moving
> away from considering him as an individual character and moving toward
> considering him as part of some larger framework. This framework may be
> moral, theological, referable to some essentially extra-literary scheme; or it
> may be referable to a part of the narrative situation itself.[46]

The characters in the parables, rather than being developed as complete
human beings, are clearly "elements which contribute to the whole" or
"parts of the plot or meaning"[47] of the stories themselves. Certainly the
masters, servants, kings, sowers of the parables are not distinguished by
their individuality. Usually they are simply described by one single trait:

the unjust judge, the unmerciful servant, the unjust steward, the wicked tenants. They are one-dimensional types whose purpose is to "contribute to the whole."

Though in the depiction of characters and in the extravagance of the plot the parables are far more illustrative or symbolic than representational, they do have a representational aspect. Many of the situations portrayed in the stories, with the exception of some details, do replicate the actual milieu of ancient Palestine in rather vivid terms. Thus in the parables we find a blending of the illustrative and the representational, the symbolic and the mimetic. Indeed one might suggest that the parables, like some other narrative works, "gain many of their effects precisely by straddling this precipitous border between the illustrative and the representational."[48] The specific effect gained by the parables is an intimation of a meaning beyond the words of the story itself. Blending the mimetic and the symbolic, the fractured realism of the parables encourages the interpreter to search for other levels of reference, to search, in terms of our two models, for the second-order signified or the unexpressed tenor of the epiphoric-type movement. The presence of the extraordinary within the ordinary, the typicality of the characters, and the indefinite tone of the stories together develop that puzzling, teasing quality that marks the parables as polyvalent forms eliciting multiple interpretations.

In this chapter we have attempted to explore some guidelines for interpretation, based on the axiom that the preservation of the integrity of the story is the principal requirement of the interpretive process. We have investigated methods for analyzing the surface structures of the parables and have discussed the possibility of clustering parables together to aid in understanding the formal patterns at work within them. Finally, we have looked at the symbolic-realistic blend, the extraordinary in the ordinary, that marks the contents of most of the stories. It remains for us to put all of this together, to demonstrate what a complete interpretation of a parable might include, and to test the value of using the configuration of the plot as both a suggestive and an evaluative criterion for interpretation.

CHAPTER V

Example:
The Parable of the Prodigal Son

"With many such parables he spoke the word to them, as they were able to hear it" (Mark 4:33). This comment by the Markan narrator proclaims both the importance of the parables and their difficulty: they are indeed bearers of "the word," but *only* as one has the ability to hear it. The parables, then as now, require their perceivers to act as interpreters who actively participate in the creation of the stories' meaning. In the last several chapters, we have been discussing both theoretically and practically the dimensions of this participation. It remains for us now to demonstrate with an example how the theoretical insights and the practical methodologies may fit together to guide an interpreter in exploring a parable in the light of modern issues and perspectives.

We have suggested that establishing what a parable meant for Jesus or for the early church, even when that is possible, does not necessarily illuminate what it can mean today. Just as the gospels themselves, the exegeses of the early and medieval church fathers, and in fact the entire long and vital homiletic traditions of the church throughout the ages have exploited the polyvalency of the parable form in order to bring "the word" to bear on the problems and concerns of each individual epoch, so the modern interpreter is faced with the same need to exploit the polyvalency of the parables in relating them to contemporary situations. In the work of his or her ancestors in the faith the interpreter finds a clear precedent for hermeneutical activity. The interpreter finds also a precedent for concern over hermeneutical excesses: Augustine condemned the exegetical extremes of Origen; Luther repudiated the medieval allegorizers; and more recently Adolf Jülicher renounced the extravagant interpretations prevalent in the eighteenth and nineteenth centuries. Hence polyvalency can be both blessing and curse. But as we have attempted to suggest, the interpreter's options need not be *either* to establish one final, normative interpretation for all time *or* to succumb to anarchy. There is a mean between the extremes. It is possible to exploit the polyvalency of the parable form while yet restricting it by taking as the first principle of interpretation the preservation of the integrity of the story itself. Understanding as fully as possible the movement and configuration of each parable story supplies both an invaluable guide for interpretations and a helpful criterion for adjudicating them.

As an example of this kind of balanced hermeneutical endeavor let us compare two interpretations of the parable of the Prodigal Son developed within the context of a literary-critical application of Freudian psychoanalytic theory. After general observations concerning the relationship of the parables to some of Freud's ideas on dream interpretation, the Prodigal Son will be explored using first Freud's discussion of mental typography and second Freud's view of emotional ambivalence. The first interpretation will be guided by and presented in conjunction with an analysis of the surface structure of the narrative. The second on the other hand will be guided only by a general apprehension of the theme of the parable. After elaborating these two readings of the parable from the same general context, we will determine whether the configuration of the plot as we have delineated it can serve as a criterion for evaluating them.

The choice of psychoanalytic theory as the context within which to view the parable reveals this particular interpreter's conviction that contemporary humanity to a greater and greater degree articulates its self-understanding in psychological terms. The vocabulary of psychology has become the vocabulary of popular culture: we discuss our "feelings," our "growth potential," our "openness," our "erogenous zones," our "oedipal resolution." Furthermore besides this influx of psychological language into the general culture, psychology has shown itself to be a serious and valuable tool for modern literary criticism. Psychological theory, and particularly psychoanalytic theory, is of course based upon the dynamics of human interaction. Therefore for a literary critic to employ these categories in exploring a literary text rather than a human being, some modifications must take place. But even with such modifications the use of psychoanalytic theory by literary critics is not an issue devoid of controversy. Many literary critics are skeptical of the usefulness of psychoanalytic categories because of the plethora of "bad" psychoanalytic criticism, criticism that has obscured and all too often bludgeoned to death the literature it was intending to enlighten, all in the name of exemplifying psychoanalytic concepts.[1] On the other hand psychoanalysts and psychologists often fault literary critics who modify psychoanalytic categories or use them with discretion and care for not being rigorous enough in their application nor far-reaching enough in their conclusions.[2] For the literary critic, however, the literature itself must always retain the central focus of attention. Using psychoanalytic models in literary criticism requires the establishment of a delicate balance between faithfulness to the psychoanalytic concepts used and unrelenting concern for the integrity of the literature being discussed. That such a balance is difficult and at times even impossible to maintain is evident; that it must always be the interpreter's goal however is mandatory. With this goal in mind let us turn to some introductory observations from psychoanalytic theory and then to two interpretations of the parable of the Prodigal Son viewed within the context of Freudian thought.

THE PARABLE AND DREAM WORK

The parable of the Prodigal Son (Luke 15:11–32), the longest of the extant parables of Jesus, has probably had a greater influence on the life of Western Christendom than any of the other parables. It has been interpreted and discussed from the time of the early church fathers to the most recent scholarship on the parables. One of the problems which appears consistently in these discussions of the Prodigal Son concerns what to do with the second section of the parable, the elder son episode (Luke 15:25–32). Some scholars have gone to the extreme position of supposing that the elder son episode was a later interpolation, though no textual evidence exists to support this view, or that it was entirely a Lukan composition. As its traditional title suggests, this parable has been understood as presenting the theme of fatherly forgiveness and mercy toward the prodigal. In the light of this theme the second episode does seem to possess a certain superfluity. The mainstream of recent research, though maintaining the linguistic and textual unity of the entire parable, still remains uncomfortable with the elder son episode. Rudolf Bultmann expresses the feeling well:

> On these grounds [the enlarging of parables by allegorical interpretations and expansions in the tradition] we may ask whether in the parable of the Prodigal Son the second part, Luke 15:25–32, is not a secondary expansion of the first, vv. 11–24. Surely the narrator's purpose, to make plain the fatherly goodness of God, which unconditionally forgives self-condemning remorse, is already attained in v. 24? And is not the point of the parable shifted when God's forgiveness is defended against the charge of injustice? Yet vv. 25–32 are not an allegorical fabrication, but remain completely within the parable so far as formal features are concerned. . . .[3]

Even in Dan O. Via, Jr.'s recent discussion of the parables from the standpoint of literary criticism, this same problem of what to do with the elder son episode arises:

From the standpoint of plot the Prodigal Son has a rounded and complete beginning, middle, and end without the elder brother episode; but . . . there are good reasons for considering the latter an original part of the parable . . . the elder brother episode—and hence the whole parable—is concluded by the father's repeating (15:32) the statement which he uttered at the end of the prodigal's story (15:24) and which expresses the movement and meaning of the latter. Thus the main interest of the story as a whole is seen to be the redemption of the prodigal.[4]

If one agrees that there are no compelling linguistic or textual grounds for dismissing the elder son episode as a later addition to the text, then any critical understanding of the text *must* deal with the totality of the parable and not just with the first half—or admit that the parable was a botched production, ill conceived and ill created. The strongest argument against the latter view of the parable is its amazing power and influence throughout centuries of Western history. The parable must speak convincingly to some deep layer of the human psyche in order for it to have maintained its prominence in the Christian tradition.

From the standpoint of literary criticism a parable presents, as we have previously indicated, a particular problem: it is more compressed and less developed than most narratives. The characters in the parables, for instance, are not characters in the Aristotelian sense of having many stereotypical and developed attributes, but rather they are agents of the action. In the Prodigal Son the only descriptive evidence we are given is that they are a father and two sons and that the father has property, servants, robes, a ring, shoes, and a fatted calf. We are not told however whether there is a mother, other children, where they live, what the father does for a living, what any of them look like—all elements we might expect in a fully mimetic or dramatic development of character, and all elements we might *need* if we intended to discuss each of the parable's "characters" as if they were living individuals.

Some psychoanalytic interpretations of the parable have collapsed precisely because they attempt to treat these "characters" as individuals. One cannot discuss, for example, the oedipal resolution of the two sons unless one assumes a great deal of material the story does not mention, not the least of which is a mother.[5] Nevertheless the parable appears to have a close formal relation to the simplest type of dream: Freud states that "condensation, together with the transformation of thoughts into situations ('dramatization'), is the most important and peculiar characteristic of dream work."[6] Moreover most dreams present in this dramatized form the fulfillment of the dreamer's unconscious wishes.[7] The characteristic narrative of a parable could easily be described as a condensed or compressed dramatization. Any work of art of course differs from a dream in that it demands a far greater amount of conscious control, thus allowing a greater amount of conscious complexity, than a dream does. Yet the parable might be viewed as a conscious and hence more complex representation of a simple wish-fulfillment type of dream with its construction based on the processes of dream work.

FIRST INTERPRETATION

In dream interpretation one often encounters the fact that various elements in the dream are all parts of a more complex unity. Another way of expressing this is to say that all the characters in the dream represent various aspects, characteristics, or desires of the dreamer. Especially when the elements in the dreamer are in conflict, the dream tends to split them into different characters or situations.[8] If we view the parable of the Prodigal Son as a type of conscious representation of a wish-fulfillment dream, then we might also see the father and two sons as elements of a complex unity. In fact the structure of the parable itself suggests this view to us. The first sentence of the story establishes a complex unity, a man with two sons (v. 11), and the second sentence begins the separation of this unity into its elements: the younger, (the elder), and the father. The rest of the parable continues the splitting process both in form and content. The division of the narrative into two distinct sections corresponds formally to the development of tension between the father and each of the two sons. Yet paradoxically at the same time that the parable continues the splitting process, it also attempts to return to the original unity of the first sentence, to bridge the dividing of "his living" (v. 12). This simultaneous presentation of the opposites disintegration/integration or splitting/unifying which the parable as a whole depicts is summed up symbolically in the central figure of the father, a point to which we shall return later.

Interestingly, the Greek word used for "his living" in verse 12b (and v. 30) is *ton bion,* rather than the more particular *ousias* of verses 12a and 13. This contrast shows that the word *bios* carries a further meaning than simply property or wealth. It connotes the whole substance and course of one's life.[9] The father was dividing the whole of his lifetime, his very being, for his sons. The wish the parable presents is the wish to reconcile these conflicting elements and restore unity. In terms of the story, the father fulfills this wish in a limited way by the end of the parable: he has unified the two sons within himself. Although the sons are not joined directly with each other as they were at the beginning of the parable, they are joined through the person of the father figure. The younger son is unified with the father by the formulaic statement in verse 24, "For this my son was dead, and is alive again; he was lost, and is found." The elder son is joined to the father by the again formulaic "all that is mine is yours" of verse 31. The father's last speech,[10] which closes the parable (vv. 31–32), states his connection with his elder son and then restates his connection with the younger son. By their individual relation to the father the two sons are indirectly joined. Thus a new, mediated unity has been established.

The unity of the parable as a whole and the parallelism of the father's attempt to reconcile each son separately with himself is suggested and confirmed not only by the motifs within the parable story that we have been discussing but also by an analysis of the structure of the surface narrative. We have not chosen to study the structure of the Prodigal Son against the background of another parable, though that might be enlightening, for the narrative of the parable itself is sufficiently long to provide some indications of its own emphases.

The Prodigal Son is an example of the parallel plot type of parable with one action (the younger son's journey) beginning and ending and then a second action (the elder son's confrontation with the father) beginning and ending. This general type of plot, as we indicated earlier, tends to encourage a comparison of the two sides with each other. Indeed in the parable of the Prodigal Son this comparison is stressed even further by a parallelism of theme and vocabulary between the two sections. The use of theme parallelism is possible in this case only because there is a concurrent parallelism in vocabulary. Analyzing the parable in terms of alternations in the manner of discourse (narrated discourse is ND, direct discourse DD) uncovers ten units, the first two setting the stage for the action and the rest dividing into parallel sections of four units each:

   I. ND: Introduction, Luke 15:11

  II. DD: Younger son's request that divides the family, v. 12a

III. ND: Younger son's journey away, vv. 12b–16
     DD: Younger son's decision to return, vv. 17–19
     ND: Father's reception of younger son, v. 20
     DD: Younger son's confession and father's response, vv. 21–24a

     ND: Elder son's return home, vv. 24b–26
     DD: Servant's explanation, v. 27
     ND: Father's reception of elder son, v. 28
     DD: Elder son's accusation and father's response, vv. 29–32

After the introductory sentence and the younger son's request set the stage for the story, the narrative falls into two main sections, the younger son's experience with the father and the elder son's experience with the father. These two sections (III) are paralleled in both theme and vocabulary. Comparing these sections with each other and investigating them in light of rhetorical style reveals the following:

III. YOUNGER SON AND FATHER	III. ELDER SON AND FATHER
a. ND: And he divided his living between them. Not many days later, the younger son gathered all he had and took his journey into a far country, and there he squandered his property in loose living. And when he had spent everything, a great famine arose in that country and he began to be in want. So he went and joined himself to one of the citizens of that country, who sent him into his <u>fields</u> (*agrous*) to feed swine. And he would gladly have fed on the pods that the swine ate; and no one gave him anything.	a'. ND: And they began to make merry. Now his elder son was in the <u>field</u> (*agrǭ*); and as he came and drew near to the house, he heard music and dancing. And he called one of the servants and asked what this meant.
b. DD: But when he came to himself he said, "How many <u>servants</u>[a] (*misthioi*) of <u>my father's</u>[b] (*patros mou*) have more than enough bread, but I perish here with hunger! I will arise and go to <u>my father</u>[b'] (*patera mou*), and I will say to him, A {["Father, I have sinned against heaven and before you; I am no longer worthy to be called your son;]} treat me as one of your <u>servants</u>[a'] (*misthiōn*)."	b'. DD: And he said, "Your brother has come, and <u>your father</u> (*pater* B {*sou*}) has [killed the fatted calf,] because he has received him safely."
c. ND: And he, arising, <u>came</u> (*ēlthen*) to <u>his father</u> (*patera heautou*). But while he was yet at a distance, <u>his father</u> (*ho pater autou*) saw him and felt compassion and running embraced him and kissed him.	c'. ND: But he was angry and was not willing <u>to come in</u> (*eiselthein*). But <u>his father</u> (*ho pater autou*) <u>coming out</u> (*exelthōn*) entreated him,

d. DD: And the son said to him,
A′ ⎧ ["Father, I have sinned against
    ⎨ heaven and before you; no longer
    ⎪ am I worthy to be called your
    ⎩ son."] But the father said to his
slaves, "Bring quickly the best
robe, and put it on him and put a
ring on his hand and shoes on his
feet; and bring the fatted calf and
kill it and let us eat and make
merry; for this my son was dead
and has come to life, was lost and
is found."

d′. DD: but he answering said to
his father, "Behold, for so many
years I have served you and I
never disobeyed your command,
but you never gave me a kid that
I might make merry with my
friends. But when this son of
yours came who has devoured
your living with prostitutes, you
B′ {[kill for him the fatted calf."]
And he said to him, "Son, you are
always with me, and all that is
mine is yours. But we had to be
merry and rejoice, for this your
brother was dead and is alive, and
was lost and is found."

The parallelism in vocabulary and theme between these two major divisions (III) of the story is evident. In the first units (a-a′) both sons are located in the fields, though the younger son's fields are in the far country, while the elder son's field is at home. The first unit of the prodigal's episode (a) is longer than that of the elder son's because it must narrate all the events which led to his eventual presence in those fields with swine. The second unit of the prodigal's adventure (b), the crucial one, is internally structured by a chiastic repetition that encompasses the son's entire speech:

$$\overset{a}{\text{servants}} \ldots \overset{b}{\text{my father}} \ldots \overset{b'}{\text{my father}} \ldots \overset{a'}{\text{servants}}.$$

This chiastic pattern, the only one in the entire parable, stresses the critical nature of this turning point in the prodigal's part of the story. Both second units (b-b′) contain parallel usages of the possessive genitive of the personal pronouns modifying the noun *father*. Moreover they are paralleled in a less obvious way: the younger son begins and ends his direct discourse with a verbal reference to servants, thinking that he would sooner be a servant than starve, while the second unit of the elder son's episode (b′) presents the direct discourse of one of those servants that the younger son wishes to become. The third units of both sections (c-c′) play on various forms of the verb *to come* in the sons' relation to their father. The younger son *comes* to his father, while the elder son refuses to *come in* so that his father must, then, *come out* to him. The final units (d-d′) of both episodes end with the repetition of the same words by the father. They also contain parallel references to killing the fatted calf and making merry. Besides ending with the same phrase, both episodes contain a parallel phrase repetition in the second unit (b-b′) and the fourth unit (d-d′). In the younger son's episode the repeated phrase is "Father, I have sinned against heaven and before you; I am no longer worthy to be called your son" (A in vv. 18b–19a and A′ in v. 21). In the corresponding units of the elder son's episode the phrase "killed the fatted calf" is repeated, though with a slight alteration in word order (B in v. 27: *ethysen . . . ton moschon ton siteuton* and B′ in v. 30: *ethysas . . . ton siteuton moschon*).

As indicators of structure these parallels in vocabulary complement and confirm the parallel motifs of the two episodes: both the younger son and the elder son travel to the house from a distance away; both are met outside by the father; both state their intentions to him outside; and with both the father has the final word. The repetition of verse 24a in verse 32 makes the final parallelism not only one of action and motif but also one of diction. The two sections of the parable are deeply intertwined, carefully paralleled thematically and structurally, to bring the listener or reader to the father's proclamation of his intimate, though different, bonds with both of his sons which he expresses in his final speech in verses 31–32.

This kind of structural analysis clearly shows the authenticity of the elder son episode: It is neither an interpolation nor an awkward addendum. It is a necessary and important part of the total configuration of the parable. We are not in this parable discussing only the forgiveness of the father for the younger son; we are also discussing the father's identification with ("all that is mine is yours," v. 31) and acceptance of the elder son. The parable as a whole, then, in both form and content is pointing toward a far more complex understanding of existence than that of the forgiveness of "self-condemning remorse."[11] It is expressing the longing of the human heart for wholeness, for a reintegration of the conflicting elements of life.

We can begin to see at this point some of the parable's appeal to people throughout the centuries. The wish to restore a unity, a harmony among the conflicting elements of one's life is an almost universal desire. Seen from this perspective the parable speaks to our deepest desire for reconciliation. Though the unity or wholeness may not be as complete as the dimly perceived harmony of the past, it is still the goal toward which we work. But the Prodigal Son's appeal reaches even further than that. It specifies some of the conflicting elements that break the unity of life.

The parable presents us with three characters, an adult and two children. The adult must mediate between the two children; he goes out of the house to talk with them, to restore them to himself (vv. 20 and 28). One of the sons has wasted himself on a dissipated life, "devoured your living with harlots" (v. 30). The other son is judgmental and unforgiving. These three elements are present in the psyche of every individual. The voice inside us which demands the fulfilling of every desire, the breaking of every taboo, is pitted against the often equally strong voice of harsh judgment on those desires. Both voices are infantile; they are the cries of children; the desires are often beyond what reality could possibly fulfill, and the judgment is often stronger and harsher than the present situation at all requires. Mediating between these two voices is the one who attempts to bring unity and harmony. The wish for unity that the parable embodies, then, repeats and represents the desire for wholeness, the resolution of conflicts within the psyche of every individual. The parable dramatizes some of the most basic conflicts and relations of the human psyche. It speaks to the wish of every individual for harmony and unity within. Let us explore briefly the three figures in the parable and their possible relation to some of the internal conflicts of human life.

The younger son figure in the parable took his part of his father's possessions and journeyed into a distant land. There he wasted his money on "loose living" (v. 13). The elder son later specifies this loose living as "devoured your living with harlots" (v. 31). The unrestrained seeking of pleasure was evidently his desire. When he ran out of money he sought familial identity with a foreigner and was subsequently sent "into his fields to feed swine." Having anything to do with swine was a religious taboo for Jews of the first century. Thus the younger son is depicted as seeking sexual pleasure and breaking religious taboos without any great concern. It is only when his desires stopped being fulfilled that as the story puts it "he came to himself." At this point in the younger son's adventures a clear contrast can be seen between his present condition and the house of his father. He is in a famine while his father has plenty; he is working in the family of a foreigner rather than being served in his father's family; he is willing to feed on swine food while in his father's house he will later feast on a fatted calf. Indeed, he is in the midst of death while life awaits his journey home. So "he came to himself." He decided to return to his father in a much more limited capacity than before in order to have "bread enough and to spare" as his father's servants did. The story presents his repentant attitude as springing not from remorse but from his desire for food to sustain himself. The picture of the younger son presented in the parable is very close to the kind of picture Freud presents of the psychic element which he terms the id. It is dominated by the unrestrained pleasure principle, and it is for the most part living in a "far country," the unconscious. It exists out of sight of the conscious mind, though to find fulfillment it must appeal to consciousness.

The theme of forgiveness usually attributed to the parable as a whole and particularly to the younger son section is far more complex than often recognized. The son proclaims the error of his ways only after luck has turned against him and he has failed to establish an alternative familial relationship. He represents the kind of conversion experience expressed by the cliché "You will never find an atheist in a foxhole." When life turns sour for him, when it becomes a living death, he returns to his father. The narrative's long and clear portrayal of the circumstances surrounding his decision to return (vv. 14–19) encourages the reader to recognize the materialistic and utilitarian basis for his "repentance." His motivation for returning to his father is given in the story, but the father's motivation for receiving him back again *before* he has even spoken his words of repentance (v. 20b) is not given. The excessive way in which the father welcomes the son moreover emphasizes the importance for the father of the son's return. It is not necessarily his repentant son he wants back but simply his son. In the context of the parable as a whole, as we have seen, the father figure's motivation is toward a reestablishment of unity, a reconciliation. What is important for the father is that the son has returned, repentant or not, changed or not, and the father's words in verses 24a and 32 underline that point. He does not require, or perhaps even desire, the reformation of his prodigal son; he only desires his return to the family: "for this my son was dead, and is alive again; he was lost, and is found."

While the narrator depicts the activities of the prodigal as "loose living" (v. 13), the elder son describes them specifically as sexual excesses: "devoured your living with harlots" (v. 30). Certainly the younger son has satisfied all his desires in the most direct way possible without regard for religious or moral taboos. Yet he is welcomed back into the family with rejoicing and feasting. The best robe, a ring, and shoes overturn the poverty of the far country; the fatted calf redeems the degradation of swine food. Moreover the elder son complains that this kind of celebration was never held for him (v. 29). It is only when the younger son returns to the family that real rejoicing takes place. In Freudian terms the unrestrained, often destructive, and wasteful desires of the id also supply much of the energy for enjoyment and the love of life so crucial to human existence. Sexuality and the search for pleasure are at the heart of human existence; their acceptance and satisfaction by the individual are crucial for health and wholeness. The father welcomes his prodigal son with an embrace and a kiss; he requires no change in his son's status or attitude before he offers his wholehearted compassion. The parable does not deny sexuality or the desire for pleasure; rather it only desires the transposition of them from the wasteful excesses of the far country to the warmth and merrymaking in the midst of the family. The younger son's desire for feasting and pleasure is still supplied in the unity of the family by the father's orders, but now the desire for pleasure is more restrained and controlled, still satisfied but not at the expense of life itself ("my son was dead, and is alive again").

Just as the younger son of the story embodies some of the aspects of Freud's conception of the id, the elder son exhibits some striking analogies with the ego ideal or "conscience." The superego, as Freud calls it, is the seat of morality, religion, law, and judgment. Its concepts however were formed during childhood and like the id do not always parallel the present reality of the adult. The elder son in the parable proclaims his righteousness to his father: "These many years I have served you, and I never disobeyed your command" (v. 29). He dissociates himself verbally from his brother and judges him harshly as one who has let his sexual desires run wild: "But when this son of yours came, who has devoured your living with harlots . . ." (v. 30). He is angry and refuses to enter the house where the celebration is going on. He presents much the type of response we often encounter from our conscience when we celebrate and "make merry."

The elder son is angry because he has been treated unfairly by his father: he is so righteous and his brother so lawless that he should be of course the more honored one; yet no feast has ever been given for him. His objection to his brother's celebration is essentially selfish, though it is rationalized in the terms of normative morality. He is angry not because his wild-living brother has been returned to the family but because he never got the kind of feast his brother is getting. To the degree that he represents the views of established religion and morality, as many commentators have observed, his presentation and stated motivations show the underside of such a rigid morality: childish selfishness and jealousy. Yet the father affirms the elder son even with his self-righteous declarations and moreover confirms the bond of identity between them: "Son, you are always with me, and all that is mine is yours" (v. 31). The father needs this son as well. As childish as the elder son's actions and statements may seem to be, he is a necessary and valued element of the family whom the father affirms and with whom he identifies. Neither sexuality nor morality are denied in the parable, but both are put under the control, judgment, and mediation of the adult, the father figure of the parable.

The parable does not tell us whether the elder son eventually comes into the house for the celebration or not. It ends with the elder son still outside, unreconciled to his brother, but his father has affirmed the bond of unity between this son and himself. Thus at the end of the narrative the full, original harmony of a man with two sons (v. 11) has not been reestablished, but a partial unification of the sons within the person of the father has been accomplished. Neither son has been presented as having fundamentally changed his nature: the elder son is still angry when we last hear from him, and the irony surrounding the younger son's "repentance" is carefully drawn in the longest, most detailed section of narration in the entire parable (vv. 13–17). The parable gives only the father the last word; we are not told how the sons respond to their father's statements either to or about them. The unity that is established within the father is a precarious one at best. Either son could disrupt it again at any moment. The harmony at the end of the parable is indeed a moment of grace, a moment when for an instant acceptance holds the field. One is reminded of a quotation from a sermon by Paul Tillich delivered at Union Seminary in New York:

> We experience moments in which we accept ourselves, because we feel that we have been accepted by that which is greater than we. If only more such moments were given to us! For it is such moments that make us love our life, that make us accept ourselves, not in our goodness and self-complacency, but in our certainty of the eternal meaning of our life. We cannot force ourselves to accept ourselves. We cannot compel anyone to accept himself. But sometimes it happens that we receive the power to say "yes" to ourselves, that peace enters into us and makes us whole, that self-hate and self-contempt disappear, and that our self is reunited with itself. Then we can say that grace has come upon us.[12]

The momentary grace of wholeness presented at the end of the parable is intimately connected with the actions of the father figure. The father in the parable is the agent of reconciliation and mediation, the one who attempts to reunite his family. As was noted above, he does not rebuke his elder son's anger just as he did not rebuke his younger son's lifestyle. He accepts them both and affirms with each of them their relation to himself. He is for a moment given the grace to say "yes" to both his sons, not because of their proclaimed righteousness nor their proclaimed repentance. Neither earns his acceptance by his father, but both receive it. The father has seen the failures of both of his sons, but he affirms their relationship anyway. It is striking to compare the actions of the father concerning the younger son with a quotation from Freud on the relation between the ego and the id:

> And he arose and came to his father. But while he was yet at a distance, his father saw him and had compassion, and ran and embraced him and kissed him [v. 20]. . . . But the father said to his servants, "Bring quickly the best robe, and put it on him, and put a ring on his hand and shoes on his feet" [v. 22].

It [the ego] offers itself, with the attention it pays to the real world, as libidinal object to the id, and aims at attaching the id's libido to itself. . . . Whenever possible it tries to remain on good terms with the id; it clothes the id's *Ucs.* [unconscious] commands with its *Pcs.* [preconscious] rationalization; it pretends that the id is showing obedience to the admonitions of reality, even when in fact it is remaining obstinate and unyielding; it disguises the id's conflicts with reality and, if possible, its conflicts with the super-ego too.[13]

For Freud the particular characteristic of the ego is "establishing the unity, or tendency to unity."[14] Yet the ego's success at this project, much like that of the father figure in the parable, is limited at best.

The ego, like the father in the parable, attempts to satisfy the demands of both the id and the superego as well as the demands of reality. It cannot ultimately change or destroy the conflicting elements within the psyche, but it can at moments mediate them and therefore modify them. So the ego's relation to the other two elements in Freud's mental typography is a complex one: on the one hand it is the rudder of the psyche, setting the direction of life, while on the other hand it is a slave to two childish and demanding masters as well as to outward reality:

In the matter of action the ego's position is like that of a constitutional monarch, without whose sanction no law can be passed but who hesitates long before imposing his veto on any measure put forward by Parliament. . . . From the other point of view, however, we see this same ego as a poor creature owing service to three masters and consequently menaced by three dangers: from the external world, from the libido of the id, and from the severity of the superego.[15]

The father is both the unifying center of the parable and its most vacillating figure. He gives in to the request of the younger son and allows him to leave; he runs out to meet first one son and then the other, something no real oriental patriarch would ever consider doing; he does not order his elder son into the house or attempt to force either son to bend to his will; in fact it is he who bends to the demands of his sons. He responds to their initiatives.

In the history of the interpretation of this parable some scholars have suggested that it be titled the Father's Love[16] rather than the Prodigal Son. Indeed one perceives something centrally important to the story in the action of the father, but at the same time there is something strangely weak in his depiction; the characters of the sons are far more strongly drawn. Yet in the course of interpreting the parable one begins to realize that in the father's weakness is his ultimate strength: because he bends to the demands of his sons he can unite them in himself. Taking a rigid position with either of his sons would destroy the possibility of wholeness forever. Yet in this strength is also his ultimate weakness: he can completely control neither of his sons, so the precarious harmony that he is momentarily able to establish can come crashing down in the next moment. The conflicts within the parable, like those within the human psyche, have not been resolved but only abated in one delicate moment of wholeness when, through the father, grace becomes a reality—but it is only for a moment.

Seen from this perspective the parable of the Prodigal Son expresses a basic human desire for unity and wholeness in life. Though the wholeness reached by and in the father at the close of the story is limited and partial, it is still a kind of resolution, perhaps the only kind life allows. Every character in the parable is necessary, including the elder son, and the conflicts and relations between them are basic to human existence. The comparison of the characters in the parable to Freud's analysis of the elements of the psyche is enlightening to the degree that Freud's analysis is an experiential reality in the lives of countless human beings. We can see that at least one reason for the parable's prominence lies in its power to touch the heart of human desire. It depicts the continuing conflict and attempt at resolution that form the basic fabric of everyday psychic life. The wish fulfilled by the parable is the wish for harmony within, for unity no matter how partial nor how precarious.

SECOND INTERPRETATION

Rather than developing a reading in conjunction with and guided by an analysis of the surface structure of the parable story, let us base this second interpretation of the Prodigal Son on a general determination of its content. Such a procedure is of course from the standpoint of this study quite wrong, but for the purpose of illustration and comparison let us ignore for the moment what we have learned concerning the importance of understanding the full configuration of the story as a guide to interpretation. We will use the same context as above, Freudian theory, and we will also presuppose our earlier discussion of the possible relation between the parable and dream work.

C. H. Dodd in describing the parable of the Prodigal Son says, "Its point would seem to lie in the contrast between the delight of a father at the return of his scapegrace son, and the churlish attitude of the 'respectable' elder brother."[17] This view of the essence of the parable draws a sharp contrast between the attitude of the father concerning the younger son and the attitude of the elder son concerning his brother. The father welcomes his prodigal son home with love, forgiveness, and rejoicing. In fact the father's reception of the son could be termed excessively loving by the standards of first-century Palestinian culture. To *run* out to his son (v. 20), as Joachim Jeremias notes, is "a most unusual and undignified procedure for an aged oriental even though he is in such haste."[18] On the other hand the elder son's response to the return of his brother is anger (v. 28). His attitude is clearly negative in the extreme: he will not go into the house to join the celebration (v. 28) and his comments about his brother are malicious and derogatory (v. 30). Responses of love on the one hand and hate on the other are directed toward the return of the younger son to his home. Just such a contrast of love with hate is described in psychoanalytic theory as emotional ambivalence: "It is particularly common to find both these [love and hate] directed simultaneously towards the same object, and this phenomenon of their co-existence furnishes the most important example of ambivalence of feeling."[19]

As we noted earlier, in interpreting dreams Freud discovered that elements of conflict within the dreamer were commonly split into separate characters or situations. The state of feeling both love and hate toward the same object is one of the most uncomfortable and disagreeable conflicts experienced by human beings. For the most part the hostile aspect of the conflict remains unconscious, while the love element is consciously expressed. In the parable of the Prodigal Son the two sides of this universal human dilemma confront each other in the figures of the father and the elder son. The younger son is a member of the family unit, one toward whom affection and special consideration should be shown by other members of that unit. However, as Freud has indicated:

> In almost every case where there is an intense emotional attachment to a particular person we find that behind the tender love there is a concealed hostility in the unconscious. This is the classical example, the prototype, of the ambivalence of human emotions. This ambivalence is present to a greater or less amount in the innate disposition of everyone.[20]

Love does not exist without hate, and the two vie as do the father and the elder son for control of the situation. The loved one has returned, but will his return be marked by anger and recriminations or by rejoicing and forgiveness? In the end the loving response governs the situation, the father talks down the anger of the elder son, but not without that anger having its say. The parable ends without a reconciliation of the hostile elder son with the younger, just as the hostile side of all emotional attachment continues to exist, though unconsciously and silently, within the individual.

The father figure and the elder son figure, those two who have remained together in the family unit, are from the perspective of this interpretation actually two sides of the same ambivalent attachment. Those impulses which collectively foster love and life and those which foster hate and destruction, according to Freud, "seldom—perhaps never—appear in isolation, but always mingle with each other in different, very varying proportions."[21] The father and the elder son are one; they are indissolubly bound to each other. The father in the parable acknowledges this identity between them by his words in verse 31: "Son, you are always with me, and all that is mine is yours." One cannot exist without the other. The conflict between the father and the elder son in the parable speaks to the painful awareness in every individual of his or her own emotional ambivalence toward those with whom attachment is most intimate and important. The wish the parable expresses is the wish to silence hostility and anger and to be conscious only of love and rejoicing: "It is fitting to make merry and be glad, for this your brother was dead, and is alive; he was lost, and is found" (v. 32).

Furthermore the details of the actions of the father and the elder son fit in amazingly well with Freud's description of emotional ambivalence. Freud postulated that hate first appears very early in a child's development in "the relation of the ego to the alien external world with its afflux of stimuli." The admixture of hate to love springs from the instinct for self-preservation.[22] In the Prodigal Son the younger son, who has left the home and journeyed into the far country, returns home as an alien, external element. He has forsaken his birthright in the family, as he himself realizes in deciding to come back home as a servant rather than as a son. He has become part of that world the elder son distrusts and abhors, the world of prostitutes (v. 30), of disobedience to the father and to religious law (vv. 15–19). His return occasions in the family unit the appearance of deep ambivalence, love for him and hate for him.

The first detail of the story that provides a clue to the emotional ambivalence which the prodigal's return elicits is the excessive nature of the father's greeting. He runs out to meet the younger son and showers him with signs of affection (vv. 20–23). Such action within the context of the Palestinian milieu can only be termed extravagant and unusual. Receiving his lost son back into the family unit could have been accomplished in a quiet and dignified manner, but that is not the story the parable relates. Here the son is met with an excessive and exaggerated demonstration of concern from the father. In fact such excessiveness itself is a sign of ambivalence. When hostility toward the loved one is present, even unconsciously, overcompensation often occurs in the form of an excessive demonstration of loving concern:

> Excessive solicitude of this kind . . . appears wherever, in addition to a predominant feeling of affection, there is also a contrary, but unconscious, current of hostility—a state of affairs which represents a typical instance of an ambivalent emotional attitude. The hostility is then shouted down, as it were, by an excessive intensification of the affection, which is expressed as solicitude and becomes compulsive, because it might otherwise be inadequate to perform its task of keeping the unconscious contrary current of feeling under repression.[23]

The excessiveness of the father's greeting prepares the way for the hostility of the elder son. This latter son was in the field when his brother returned and hence was unconscious of the events taking place at the house, but that state of affairs ends quickly.

Once informed of the events that had occurred, the elder son responds in anger. When his father comes out to entreat him to join the celebration he articulates the reason for this hostility. On the basis of the interpretation we are developing we might expect the elder son to claim that the return of the prodigal is the basis for his hostility. That he does not do. Instead he blames his anger on the fact that the father has not killed for him the fatted calf so that he might party with his friends (vv. 29–30). He is not, evidently, upset that his brother has returned but only that he has never been given a party like this one. However, Freud's description of emotional ambivalence provides some insight into the elder son's contention: when unconscious hostile impulses occasionally reach consciousness, they have often been affected by the mechanism of displacement:

> An unconscious impulse need not have arisen at the point where it makes its appearance; it may arise from some quite other region and have applied originally to quite other persons and connections.[24]

The elder son cannot consciously express his hatred and anger toward the return of his brother; therefore he displaces the anger he feels toward his brother onto the failure of his father to provide a party for him. Furthermore very often in the case of displacement the particular act associated with the displaced hatred represents a hostile act one would like to perform against the loved person.[25] The elder son emphasizes that he is angry because: "You never gave me a kid, that I might make merry with my friends" (v. 29). For him to "make merry," the elder son needs to "kill the fatted calf." The act of killing the calf may represent by displacement the elder son's desire to kill his younger brother. The conscious expression of this negative side of emotional ambivalence has undergone displacement, but the displacement itself witnesses to the murderous impulses it at the same moment attempts to hide. In the elder son we see an example of the displaced hostility and hatred that form the underside of love and affection.

Viewed from this perspective the parable of the Prodigal Son details and examines the painful nature of emotional ambivalence. The parable fulfills the wish to silence and overcome the hatred and murderous hostility that is inextricably interwoven with the deepest love and concern. The parable ends as we wish all such deplorable conflicts would: love silences hatred, joy suppresses anger. The father has the final word: "It was fitting to make merry and be glad, for this your brother was dead, and is alive; he was lost, and is found" (v. 32).

EVALUATION

We have now examined two interpretations of the parable of the Prodigal Son within the context of psychoanalytic theory. Before proceeding to an evaluation of their differences let us consider for a moment what they share in common: their general context. Undoubtedly a few other interpretations of this parable within a Freudian context might be established, though the context itself imposes a limit on their number. Using a system as complex and extensive as psychoanalytic theory for the parable's context permits a greater number of different interpretations than other, more limited contexts would. In employing such a system the interpreter is not required to involve the whole scheme in any one interpretation; that in fact would be an impossibility. It is necessary, however, that the interpreter represent whatever elements of the whole he or she chooses as fully and faithfully as possible. Not only the integrity of the text but also the integrity of the contextual system must be preserved. To describe, for instance, Freud's conception of the superego as a benevolent and forgiving psychic element in order to fit it into a particular interpretation is clearly inapt. Inapt too is the supermarket approach to interpretation, in which the interpreter takes a little from this constellation (e.g., comparing the id and the younger son) and combines it with a little from that constellation (e.g., comparing the father and elder son with the appearance of emotional ambivalence) to make one final reading. Either of these two procedures would violate the integrity of the contextual system itself.

Whatever contextual system is chosen—be it psychological, sociological, theological, economic, or philosophical—it must not only be employed faithfully but it must also be itself open to evaluation. If the context is suspect, so then is the final interpretation. Freudian psychoanalytic theory is certainly not without detractors. Nor, however, is it without defenders. Some wish to amend, revise, or abolish it, while others continue to assert its unqualified superiority.[26] Whether or not psychoanalysis as a therapeutic method excels other similar methods is not a debate we wish to enter—nor, in fact, is it a debate with particular relevance for the literary-critical use of psychoanalytic concepts. The use of psychoanalytic theory as a basis for psychological interpretation, however, recommends itself on at least three grounds: it remains the most comprehensive, logical, and cohesive theoretical study of human psychology; it is the foundation, even if negatively, of most contemporary psychological systems; and it has been the subject of many philosophical and scientific critiques, providing it with immense amounts of secondary material that can be of assistance to an interpreter. Hence employing Freudian psychoanalytic theory as the context for interpretation is a defensible choice for one wishing to relate the parables to the contemporary interest in psychological development.

The two interpretations of the Prodigal Son presented in this chapter share the same general context; how then do they differ? They of course utilize different aspects of the contextual system, but their differences are more profound than that. Indeed the process of interpretation in each case begins from different standpoints: the first, from a careful exploration of the surface structure of the parable; the second, from a general estimation of its "point." We have argued in the preceding chapters that exploiting the polyvalency of the parable form is a necessary and important endeavor for the contemporary hermeneut, that in fact in so doing she or he follows the example of countless ancestors in the faith, including the gospel writers themselves. However, we have also proposed that the polyvalency of the parables, their openness to multiple interpretations, requires some restriction in order to avoid anarchy. Such a restriction is supplied, we suggested, by affirming as the first principle of interpretation the preservation of the integrity of the text. The total configuration of the parable story itself, then, becomes both the guide and evaluative criterion for interpretation. The appropriateness or inappropriateness of an interpretation is always an arguable issue. As Paul Ricoeur says, "An interpretation must not only be probable, but more probable than another interpretation."[27] In order to argue more cogently for the structure of the text as the primary interpretive guide, we have articulated two probable readings of the Prodigal Son to compare with each other. Our contention is that the first interpretation, that guided by and developed along with an exploration of the surface structure of the parable, is more probable and more appropriate to the story than the second one.

The exploration of the surface structure of the Prodigal Son indicated clearly that in form the parable developed separately the story of the younger son (Luke 15:11–24) from that of the elder son (vv. 25–32). The father was part of both stories, ending each with the same words. The structure of the parable suggested the comparison of the younger and elder sons, with the father as mediator. The first interpretation, using Freud's mental typography as the specific context, compared and contrasted the two sons in relation to the father, pointing to similarities with the relation of the id and superego to the ego in Freudian theory. Hence the content of the first interpretation matched the form of the parable itself.

In the second interpretation, employing Freud's discussion of emotional ambivalence, the point of the parable was taken to be the conflicting responses of the father and elder son to the younger son's return. The father and elder son corresponded in this reading to the loving and hating aspects of emotional attachment. They formed, then, two sides of the same response. However, this contrast between the father and elder son is not represented in the structure of the parable itself. The father is present in both episodes of the story, but the elder son appears only in the last. The father confronts and speaks with both other characters; the elder son speaks only to one. Formally the presentations of the father and the elder son are asymmetric rather than symmetric as the content, construed by the second interpretation, would suggest. Thus in the first interpretation form and content correspond, but in the second they do not. The second interpretation, then, violates the axiomatic inseparability of form and content.

Furthermore in the first interpretation the actions of each figure in the story were utilized fully. The explication of the correspondence between the id and the younger son depended upon the details of his story for its effectiveness; his journey into the far country, his financial and sexual excesses, his breaking of religious taboos, his belly orientation, his ultimate return to the father for the satisfaction of his needs—all are related to Freud's characterization of the id. Similarly the depictions of the father and elder son were fully explored in relation to the ego and superego concepts. Thus the first interpretation required the whole of the story told by the parable; no part of it could be omitted.

The second interpretation, however, focused mainly on the father and elder son; the details of the younger son's story were unnecessary for its elaboration. The younger son was characterized simply as the alien external element. None of the details of his story, his feeding swine, his hunger, his wasting his money, were actually required. For the second interpretation the parable could just as well have begun: "A son, who had been away for a time, returned to his home. But while he was yet at a distance, his father saw him. . . ." Ironically, this contemporary interpretation of the Prodigal

Son within the context of emotional ambivalence reverses the traditional trend in reading the parable; rather than focusing mainly on the younger son's episode and essentially omitting the elder son's episode, it focuses upon the elder son and essentially omits the younger. Hence the second interpretation not only violates the inseparability of form and content but it also fits only one-half of the parable narrative. The second interpretation does not preserve the integrity of the parable story.

Thus we can see from the example of these two interpretations the importance of understanding as fully as possible the total configuration of the parable story as a guide to interpretation. The first interpretation, guided by an analysis of the surface structure, must be judged a more appropriate and probable reading of the parable of the Prodigal Son than the second one. All in all, this example demonstrates that the theoretical and practical elements of this study can fit together to assist the modern interpreter in creatively exploiting the polyvalency of the parable form with restraint and care.

Conclusion

This study began by observing the diversity of interpretations found in parable scholarship since Adolf Jülicher, though it could just as easily have remarked such variety in any epoch including that of the gospel writers themselves. From this observation of multiple interpretations we moved to a consideration of the parable form itself, hoping to discover the basis of its polyvalency. By exploring two models for the parable, a semiotic one and a rhetorical one, the indeterminate or dependent nature of the form was disclosed. Moreover we learned that its dynamic indeterminacy compels interpretation, that the context within which a parable is viewed profoundly affects its meaning, and that the interpreter, by providing the focus through which the world view of the story is understood, becomes in fact its cocreator.

Fearing that the polyvalent nature of the parables would lead to anarchy, we discussed the possibility of reading them solely within their gospel contexts. Such a plan, however, raised as many problems as it alleviated, for the gospel settings themselves often violated the integrity of the parable stories. Yet limiting them to their gospel contexts did restrict the range of interpretations any individual parable could bear. But this restriction was founded upon concerns vital to the first-century Christian community and not to the present situation of twentieth-century life. Thus we suggested that rather than holding fast to the actual interpretations articulated by the gospel writers, we should instead follow their example of hermeneutical activity. Just as they exploited the polyvalency of the parable form to bring the word to bear on issues of concern for the early church, so we also must exploit it in order to confront the various problems of the modern church. In such exploitation, however, the possibility of anarchy still loomed.

To prevent anarchy while yet exploiting polyvalency, we proposed that the first principle of interpretation must be the preservation of the integrity of the parable story itself. Once the full configuration of that story is known,

115

it functions both as a guide to interpretations and as an evaluative criterion for them. We then studied two methods for analyzing the surface structure of the narratives, an explication of manner of discourse and of rhetorical style, that were based upon the axiomatic inseparability of form and content. Finally, to observe the value of understanding the full configuration of the text in practice, we expounded and evaluated two interpretations of the parable of the Prodigal Son. In so doing we discovered that the reading guided by an exploration of the surface structure of the narratives was far more successful at preserving the integrity of the story than was the one guided only by a general apprehension of its point. Thus our proposed first principle of interpretation did indeed effectively restrict the range of probable and appropriate interpretations while yet encouraging the work of the modern hermeneut in exploiting the polyvalency of the parables.

Each chapter of this study was introduced by a verse from the gospels concerning the parables which proved to be as germane to the modern world as to the ancient:

> To you it has been given to know the secrets of the kingdom of God; but for others they are in parables, so that seeing they may not see, and hearing they may not understand.   —Luke 8:10

> Let the one who has ears to hear, hear.   —Mark 4:9

> What is the kingdom of God like? And to what shall I compare it?
>   —Luke 13:18

> He did not speak to them without a parable, but privately to his own disciples he explained everything.   —Mark 4:34

> And how will you understand all the parables?   —Mark 4:13

> With many such parables he spoke the word to them, as they were able to hear it.   —Mark 4:33

The attempt to hear the word of the kingdom of God spoken in parables unites the modern hermeneut with generations of ancestors in the faith. No consensus or unanimity of opinion has ever tainted this long and illustrious progression of interpreters. Indeed, to plumb the "secrets of the kingdom" is the challenge that the parables present anew to each successive era. And the measure of those depths has yet to be fully reckoned—if ever it can.

Notes

INTRODUCTION

1. Most of the English quotations from the Bible found throughout this work are from the Revised Standard Version (RSV). Those quotations which are not from the RSV are my own translations.

2. Paul Ricoeur, *Interpretation Theory* (Fort Worth: Texas Christian University Press, 1976), p. 74.

CHAPTER I:
The Problem of Multiple Interpretations

1. See Rudolf Bultmann, *History of the Synoptic Tradition,* trans. John Marsh (New York: Harper & Row, 1963), p. 199.

2. The question of definition of any genre is a very complex one. To deal with all the issues involved in a theoretical discussion of what a parable is would be far beyond the scope of this present study. For a discussion of some of the elements involved in such a study see Norman Petersen, "On the Notion of Genre in Via's 'Parable and Example Story: A Literary-Structuralist Approach,'" *Semeia* 1 (1974): 134–81.

3. Bultmann, pp. 174–79.

4. Adolf Jülicher, *Die Gleichnisreden Jesu,* 2 vols. (Tübingen: J.C.B. Mohr [Paul Siebeck], 1888–99).

5. Bultmann, p. 174.

6. Ibid. C. H. Dodd was the first to question seriously the categories set down by Jülicher and Bultmann. Dodd still drew a distinction between a parable and a similitude, though noting that the line between them was not precise, but he discarded the category of example story. *The Parables of the Kingdom,* 3rd ed. (New York: Scribner's, 1961), pp. 5–7. Cf. Joachim Jeremias's evaluation of the failure of form-critical categories for the parables, in *The Parables of Jesus,* trans. S. H. Hooke (London: SCM Press; New York: Scribner's, 1972), pp. 20–21.

7. Bultmann, p. 178.

8. John Dominic Crossan, *In Parables: The Challenge of the Historical Jesus* (New York: Harper & Row, 1973), pp. 57–66.

9. Dan O. Via, Jr., "Parable and Example Story: A Literary-Structuralist Approach," and Crossan, "Parable and Example in the Teaching of Jesus" and "Structuralist Analysis and the Parables of Jesus," all in *Semeia* 1 (1974): 105–33, 63–104, and 192–221.

10. For an excellent and very complete discussion of this exchange see Norman Perrin, *Jesus and the Language of the Kingdom* (Philadelphia: Fortress Press, 1976), pp. 168–81.

11. Crossan, *In Parables,* pp. 64–65.

12. The first volume of Jülicher's work contained his theoretical arguments. Volume 2, which appeared eleven years later, presented interpretations that reflected his application of theoretical principles to individual parable stories.

13. E.g., Dodd; Jeremias; Eta Linnemann, *Jesus of the Parables,* trans. John Sturdy (New York: Harper & Row, 1966); Via, *The Parables: Their Literary and Existential Dimension* (Philadelphia: Fortress Press, 1967); and Crossan, *In Parables.*

14. E.g., Jack Dean Kingsbury, *The Parables of Jesus in Matthew 13: A Study in Redaction-Criticism* (Richmond: John Knox Press, 1969); Charles E. Carlston, *The Parables of the Triple Tradition* (Philadelphia: Fortress Press, 1975); Kenneth E. Bailey, *Poet and Peasant: A Literary-Cultural Approach to the Parables in Luke* (Grand Rapids: Eerdmans Publishing Co., 1976).

15. See Albert Schweitzer, *The Quest of the Historical Jesus* (New York: Macmillan Co., 1968). Schweitzer presents an excellent summary and critique of many of the nineteenth-century lives of Jesus.

16. See James M. Robinson, *A New Quest of the Historical Jesus* (London: SCM Press, 1959).

17. Amos Wilder, *Early Christian Rhetoric: The Language of the Gospel,* rev. ed. (Cambridge: Harvard University Press, 1971), p. 85.

18. Jeremias, pp. 23–114. In this section Jeremias explains what elements he determined to be additional expansions and why.

19. Although it is true that all historical data are to some extent hypothetical, it seems to me important to make distinctions based on the degree of probability behind various historical reconstructions. The reconstruction of the general cultural and social milieu of first-century Palestine is a hypothetical historical datum with a high degree of probability. Furthermore the reconstruction in general terms of the message of the historical Jesus or the various Christologies of the early church are hypothetical historical data with moderate degrees of probability. However, the reconstruction of the *ipsissima verba* of Jesus, the original spoken parables, would seem to me to be hypothetical formulations with a rather low degree of probability. The critical assessments of degrees of probability behind historical data must be based on many factors, the most important being the availability, diversity, clarity, and accuracy of the sources, and the historical assumptions used to draw conclusions from those sources. To question the value of hypothetical reconstructions of *Ur*-parable texts is in no way to deny the validity and importance of historical criticism generally for the study of New Testament materials. Indeed historical criticism is indispensable.

20. Wilder; Via, *Parables;* Robert Funk, "The Parable as Metaphor," in *Language, Hermeneutic, and the Word of God* (New York: Harper & Row, 1966); Perrin.

21. Via, *Parables,* pp. 177–205.

22. Kingsbury, p. 10. Cf. Willie Marxsen, "Redaktionsgeschichtliche Erklärung der sogenannten Parabeltheorie des Markus," *Zeitschrift für Theologie und Kirche* 52 (1955): 255–71; W. Wilkens, "Die Redaktion des Gleichniskapitels Mark 4 durch Matth," *Theologische Zeitschrift* 20 (1964): 304–27; and Madeleine Boucher, *The Mysterious Parable: A Literary Study* (Washington: Catholic Biblical Association of America, 1977), pp. 42–85.

23. Carlston, p. xii.

24. Ibid., p. 172. Cf. also pp. 116, 154, 160–61, 166–67. Carlston's book is an excellent compendium of critical studies on the parables but is itself flawed by a critical omission in methodology. This major methodological problem has to do with Carlston's attempts to determine the authenticity of the material. From where

and how is he drawing his knowledge of the life and teachings of Jesus to which he compares the parable texts? He does not argue for an overall view of the ministry of Jesus, nor does he compare the parables with other texts within the New Testament that have been argued by others to be authentic material. What Carlston does most often is to refer to a quotation from Jeremias or Jülicher or some other scholar which says Jesus did this or Jesus believed that. These quotations, then, become the norm for judging whether parabolic material is authentic or not. Cf., e.g., p. 160 where Jesus' understanding of the kingdom is determined by reference to Eberhard Jüngel, Jülicher, Dodd, and Jeremias without regard for the fact that each of these scholars' overall view of the message and teaching of Jesus varies radically from the views held by the others.

25. Bailey, p. 83.

26. Ibid., p. 26. Bailey's intent is quite commendable, but he does not succeed in fulfilling it because the methodologies he develops are amazingly naïve in both the cultural and literary aspects of his study. The problem with his literary-critical method will be discussed further in Chapter IV, but suffice it to say here that his understanding of literature is idiosyncratic and definitely problematic, as this quotation illustrates: "Rather than looking, as Via has done, for 'comic,' 'tragic,' 'the protagonist's power of action,' and 'plot,' Eastern literature must be examined using its own literary art forms. Then when the question is asked, 'What are the primary literary art forms in Eastern literature?' the almost exclusive answer is, 'Stories and poems'" (pp. 25–26). Evidently for Bailey Eastern stories, whatever they might be, do not have plots and protagonists. Surely this is a strange theory of literature.

The cultural aspect of Bailey's study is called "oriental exegesis" (p. 29), which involves in part Bailey's own attempt to discuss the parables with present-day Middle Eastern people. Since the life of the contemporary Middle Eastern peasant is "remarkably archaic" (p. 31), this peasant can give Bailey some understanding of what the parable meant to people in the time of Jesus. Whether this theoretical assertion about the nature of present-day peasants is true or not, Bailey's practical methodology calls into question the whole plan. Of the twenty-five resource people Bailey talks to, "the majority . . . are Arab pastors who themselves have wrestled with the text" (p. 36). Surely a man who has been trained as a pastor could not be considered an ordinary, "remarkably archaic" peasant. Further, the very fact that most if not all of the resource people are Christians suggests that their response to New Testament material might be influenced by interpretations of it they have heard in their churches, giving them a definite bias that the first hearers of the parables would not have had. Bailey as an anthropologist is suspect indeed.

27. See Perrin, pp. 89–193; Kingsbury, "The Parables of Jesus in Current Research," *Dialog* 11 (Spring 1972): 101–7; Carlston, "Changing Fashions in Interpreting the Parables," *Andover Newton Quarterly* 14 (March 1974): 227–33; for a brief review of parable research before Jülicher see G. V. Jones, *The Art and Truth of the Parables* (London: S.P.C.K., 1964), pp. 3–26.

28. *Die Gleichnisreden Jesu.*

29. Ibid., 2:276, 467, 596.

30. Dodd, p. 144.

31. Jeremias, p. 152.

32. The term *valid* is not being used in any technical sense. It denotes here simply its dictionary meaning of "well-founded" or "sound" (OED). The problem of technical validity in interpretation is a vexing one on all fronts. Does a literary work have only one meaning, and if it does, how can that meaning be determined

so that all interpretations of the work can be judged by it? The literary, linguistic, and philosophical study of semantics is at this time so inchoate and divisive that no definitive answer to either part of the question is possible. What limited criteria are available for judging various interpretations as valid or not in the particular case of parables will be discussed in Chapter IV. For an important contribution to the ongoing discussion of questions of validity in interpretation see E. D. Hirsch, *Validity in Interpretation* (New Haven: Yale University Press, 1967), and for a recent refutation of Hirsch see Paul Ricoeur, "Construing and Constructing," *London Times Literary Supplement*, 25 February 1977, p. 216. For a general discussion of Hirsch's position and its weaknesses see Richard E. Palmer, *Hermeneutics* (Evanston: Northwestern University Press, 1969), pp. 60–71.

33. Jeremias, pp. 113–14.

34. Ibid., p. 114.

35. The major exception to this rule is Crossan, who in most of his discussions attempts to reformulate the original parable text for himself rather than relying upon Jeremias's work. This procedure, which impressively illustrates his ability as a historical critic, accords with his desire, similar to that of Jeremias, to reach the original words of Jesus. See *In Parables*, pp. 4–7, 35. For a further discussion of *Ur*-parable texts see Chapter IV, pp. 72–73.

36. For a further discussion of allegorical interpretation as a hermeneutical methodology see Chapter III, pp. 63–65.

37. Eberhard Jüngel thinks that Jülicher's distinction actually comes from Aristotle's *Logic* rather than the *Rhetoric*. See Jüngel's *Paulus und Jesus* (Tübingen: J.C.B. Mohr, 1962), pp. 91–92.

38. *In Parables*, pp. 8–10. Since writing *In Parables* Crossan himself has changed his position on allegory. He now sees allegory as a valid concept for use in parable interpretation. See *Semiology and Parables*, ed. Daniel Patte (Pittsburgh: Pickwick Press, 1976), pp. 264–78.

39. *In Parables*, p. 15.

40. Ibid.

41. The term *allegory* itself confuses the issue because it has, I think, at least three discernible meanings in general use: first, allegory is used to mean the method of allegorical interpretation which began with the Stoics and reached its height in the late Middle Ages; second, allegory is commonly used to describe that genre of literature written under the influence of the allegorical interpretational method in which the author intended his work to be understood allegorically; and third, allegory is used, very much as metaphor has been used in recent theoretical discussions, as a metalinguistic term denoting the ability of language to function referentially. In this third realm of meaning allegory and metaphor are indeed intimately connected concepts. To say that the parables contain allegorical elements is simply to say that they work by sets of correspondences, but it is not necessarily to say that the author of the parables *intended* to write allegories (i.e., the second usage discussed above), a fact which at this time would be impossible to discover. The failure to make such distinctions in the use of the word *allegory* can result in confused and misleading interpretations like that of Madeleine Boucher who in *The Mysterious Parable: A Literary Study* defines allegory as "*simply a device of meaning, and not in itself a literary form or genre . . .* [for] it appears in literary works of many kinds" (p. 20, italics hers). Using Boucher's method of determining the definition of allegory we would have to conclude that fable, biography, and history, to name but a few, are also simply devices of meaning and not literary genres. The fact that it is possible to write a fabulous novel

or a biographical novel or a historical novel, however, does not prohibit one from also writing works that could be classified formally as a fable, a biography, and a history.

A reevaluation of the place of allegory in parable research in terms of the third meaning suggested above would mean practically that the interpreter could no longer simply assume that an element which she or he believes to be allegorical can be expunged from the text as a later accretion even if the logic of the story suggests that the element be retained. Assumed allegorical tendencies alone could no longer be the final acid test for traditional expansions of the text. The method of establishing the text of the parable, if that is what one wishes to do, which would result from this reevaluation of allegory would be a great deal messier and more tentative than before, but probably ultimately more realistic, for though it is true that the early church at times tended to add allegorical elements to the parable texts, that does not mean that some were not present from the beginning, especially where the logic of the narrative itself suggests their existence. An excellent, recent discussion of allegory is found in Michael Murrin, *The Veil of Allegory* (Chicago: University of Chicago Press, 1969); also cf. C. S. Lewis, *Allegory of Love* (London: Oxford University Press, 1936) for a presentation of the English "psychological" school of allegory, and Angus Fletcher, *Allegory: The Theory of a Symbolic Mode* (Ithaca: Cornell University Press, 1964) for a more recent and sophisticated restatement of that approach. On allegory as an interpretive system see Morton Bloomfield, "Allegory as Interpretation," *New Literary History* 3 (Winter 1972): 301–17.

42. Murrin's development of the relationship between allegory and prophecy is particularly enlightening and thought-provoking. Murrin, pp. 21–53.

43. Wilder, pp. 79–96.

44. The term *literary criticism* here and throughout this study refers to principles developed for the general study of literature and not to the special use of that term found in biblical scholarship of the last century, describing a kind of composition criticism or source criticism.

45. Jones, p. 165 (italics his).

46. Funk, pp. 133–62.

47. Though Crossan's book *In Parables* contains an extensive discussion of literary theory, his historical concerns are predominant. It is often difficult to see how Crossan's literary theory affects his actual interpretation of individual parables.

48. Jones, p. 204.

49. Via, *Parables*, p. 174.

50. Via, "The Prodigal Son: A Jungian Reading," *Semeia* 9 (1977): 33.

51. I have omitted from this overview both the work of Ernst Fuchs, Jüngel, and Linnemann on the "new hermeneutic" view of parables and a full review of Crossan's recent book *In Parables*. Neither of these would contribute much to the line of argument being developed, though they also do not detract from it. Fuchs et al. stimulated much discussion among scholars for a time but ultimately failed to produce a very cogent theory. For an excellent review and evaluation of the "new hermeneutic" school see Perrin, pp. 107–27. For a discussion of Fuchs's own interpretation of parables see Kingsbury, "Ernst Fuchs' Existentialist Interpretation of the Parables," *Lutheran Quarterly* 22 (1970): 380–95. Crossan's book *In Parables*, though containing an exposition of some literary theory, mainly attempts a historical reconstruction of the Jesus of the parables comparable to the kind of work done by Jeremias and Dodd; for Crossan, however, the message of Jesus is more Heideggerian and literary than eschatological. Cf. Perrin, pp. 155–68.

52. A.-J. Greimas, *Sémantique structural: Recherche de méthode* (Paris: Larousse, 1966).

53. Via, "Parable and Example Story," pp. 118–19.

54. Crossan, "Structural Analysis," pp. 202–6.

55. See Perrin's comments on the confusion arising from these structuralist analyses, Perrin, pp. 174–76. While the intent of this section has been to explore the incidence of multiple interpretations of the same parable using the same method, Perrin's book (see pp. 88–181) documents in detail the radically different interpretations of the same parable (specifically, the Good Samaritan) that can arise when scholars are employing different methodological assumptions.

CHAPTER II:
Two Models for the Parable Form

1. The presence of multiple interpretations is not of course a problem limited to the parables. Most literature seems to be capable of generating a variety of interpretations, and literary critics have been much exercised recently over attempts to develop just such a metacritical system as we are postulating here. Cf. E. D. Hirsch, *Validity in Interpretation* (New Haven: Yale University Press, 1967) and articles in *New Literary History* vol. 3 (Winter 1972) and vol. 4 (Spring 1973).

2. In linguistics and philosophy see, e.g., Max Black, *Models and Metaphors* (Ithaca: Cornell University Press, 1962) and Frederick Ferré, *Language, Logic, and God* (New York: Harper & Row, 1961); in theology see, e.g., David Tracy, *Blessed Rage for Order* (New York: The Seabury Press, 1975).

3. Black, p. 222. Black goes on to distinguish "theoretical models," used extensively in scientific research, but discussion of them has been omitted here because they are not germane to the argument.

4. Tracy, p. 22.

5. Mary Ann Tolbert, "The Prodigal Son: An Essay in Literary Criticism from a Psychoanalytic Perspective," pp. 1–20; Dan O. Via, Jr., "The Prodigal Son: A Jungian Reading," pp. 21–43; and Bernard B. Scott, "The Prodigal Son: A Structuralist Interpretation," pp. 45–73, all in *Semeia* 9 (1977).

6. Susan Wittig, "A Theory of Multiple Meanings," *Semeia* 9 (1977): 76 (italics hers).

7. Ibid., p. 79. Cf. Ferdinand de Saussure, *Course in General Linguistics,* ed. Charles Bally and Albert Sechehaye (New York: McGraw-Hill, 1959).

8. Wittig, "The Historical Development of Structuralism," *Soundings* 58 (Summer 1975): 146, 163.

9. Ibid., p. 163.

10. Jonathan Culler, *Structuralist Poetics* (Ithaca: Cornell University Press, 1975), p. 6.

11. Ibid., p. 4.

12. Roland Barthes, *Elements of Semiology,* trans. from the French by Annette Lavers and Colin Smith (Boston: Beacon Press, 1967), p. 39.

13. Barthes, *Mythologies,* trans. from the French by Annette Lavers (New York: Hill and Wang, 1972), p. 113.

14. Wittig, "Multiple Meanings," p. 84. Wittig's reference to events in "extra-linguistic reality" is puzzling. The comment does not follow from her preceding arguments, nor does it affect her conclusions. Because of the murky connotations such a statement raises about a postulated historical basis for the parable stories I choose to disregard it in my further discussions of her work.

15. Ibid., p. 85.

16. Ibid., pp. 84–85 (italics hers). Although Wittig states clearly her view that parabolic signs are part of a duplex semiotic, she does not state *why* that should be so. She does not show, in other words, what it is in the parables themselves that suggests the existence of an indeterminate second-order signified. I would fill in this lacuna in her argument by citing the common characteristics of parables discussed in the last chapter: the extraordinary in the ordinary and the indefinite tone of the stories. These two characteristics force one to seek meaning beyond the denotation of the parabolic sign itself; they encourage the search for a second-order signified.

17. Barthes, *Mythologies*, pp. 114–16. Wittig in conversation disagreed with Barthes's implication that all second-order systems are myths. She does not think the parables are mythic.

18. Wittig, "Multiple Meanings," p. 87.

19. Ibid. (italics hers).

20. Ibid., pp. 87–88.

21. Ibid., pp. 88–89.

22. Ibid., p. 96 (italics hers).

23. Paul Ricoeur, "Structure, Word, Event," trans. Robert Sweeney in *The Conflict of Interpretations* (Evanston: Northwestern University Press, 1974), p. 80.

24. See the careful review of the failure of Roman Jakobson's poetic analysis and A.-J. Greimas's structural semantics in Culler, *Poetics*, pp. 55–95. Culler's criticism of Greimas suggests not only a failure in practice but a failure in principle: "It may be impossible in principle as well as in practice, to construct a model which would derive the meaning of a text or of a set of texts from the meaning of lexical items" (p. 85). Cf. Via, *Kerygma and Comedy in the New Testament* (Philadelphia: Fortress Press, 1975), pp. 28–31, where Via debates between the linguistic claims of structuralism and literary criticism but manages to come down solidly on the fence: "What is true at the level of the sentence may not be true for the text as a whole. But then again it might be" (p. 31).

25. Culler, p. 31. Cf. also p. 109: "Linguistics does not . . . provide a method for the interpretation of literary works. It may provide a general focus, either suggesting to the critic that he look for differences and oppositions which can be correlated with one another and organized as a system which generates the episodes or forms of the text, or offering a set of concepts in which interpretations may be stated. Both cases have their dangers." See Robert Scholes, *Structuralism in Literature* (New Haven: Yale University Press, 1974), for a literary critic who uses these two "cases" and most of the time recognizes their limitations: for example, "What, then, has structuralism to offer us that will help in the practical criticism of poetic texts? I believe it has much to offer, but only in an indirect manner" (p. 39).

26. Culler, p. 25.

27. Wittig, "Multiple Meanings," p. 92.

28. Ibid., p. 97.

29. The classical background of the term *rhetoric* is heterogeneous. Prior to Aristotle's definition of rhetoric as the art of discovering all means of persuasion, the Sophists and Isocrates had propounded it generally as the art of speech or oratory, with the art of persuasion being specifically taught under the rubric of dialectics (see H. I. Marrou, *A History of Education in Antiquity*, trans. George Lamb [London: Sheed and Ward, 1956], pp. 51–52, 84–87). Though Aristotle's view of rhetoric as persuasion was influential, major segments of the ancient world

continued to use the term *rhetoric* in the more general sense of the rules and conventions of oratory. For instance Augustine, quoting Cicero, "the author of Roman eloquence," cites the three ends of rhetoric: to teach, to delight, and to persuade, each of which required a particular style of speaking (in *De doctrina Christiana* 4.17). This conventional use of rhetoric, moreover, underlies the rhetorical handbooks of the ancient and medieval schools (see Marrou, pp. 284–91 and 340–50). Hence the term *rhetoric* in the ancient and medieval worlds could refer specifically to the art of persuasion or more broadly to the rules of oratory or eloquence, in which persuasion figured as but one of several ends. Contemporary understandings of rhetoric evince a similar heterogeneity. The conception of rhetoric as the art of persuasion, for example, guides Wayne Booth's study of those aspects of literature specifically designed to affect the audience (see *The Rhetoric of Fiction* [Chicago: University of Chicago Press, 1961] and *A Rhetoric of Irony* [Chicago: University of Chicago Press, 1974]). A more general conception of rhetoric as the rubrics of speech is present in the philosophical discussion of rhetorical tropes, found in, for example, I. A. Richards, *The Philosophy of Rhetoric* (London: Oxford University Press, 1936). From this latter stream my use of the term *rhetoric* is drawn.

For the seventeenth-century decline of rhetoric as literary criticism and the nineteenth-century attack upon it by Benedetto Croce see William K. Wimsatt and Cleanth Brooks, *Literary Criticism: A Short History* (New York: Random House, 1957), pp. 244–47 and 512–13.

30. See, e.g., Black; I. A. Richards; Philip Wheelwright, *Metaphor and Reality* (Bloomington: Indiana University Press, 1962); idem, *The Burning Fountain* (Bloomington: Indiana University Press, 1968); and Douglas Berggren, "The Use and Abuse of Metaphor," *The Review of Metaphysics* 16 (1962–63): 237–58 and 450–72 for an excellent critical description and evaluation of the "theory of metaphorical tension." Throughout the succeeding discussion my conception of metaphor is also indebted to the work of Ricoeur, *La métaphore vive* (Paris: Editions du Seuil, 1975).

31. C. H. Dodd, *The Parables of the Kingdom,* 3rd ed. (New York: Scribner's, 1961), p. 5.

32. The term *rhetorical* in this section refers only to the classical status of metaphor as a trope or figure of rhetoric. It is not related to the discipline of biblical criticism expounded by James Muilenburg that is called rhetorical criticism; for a further discussion of the latter see Chapter IV.

33. See, e.g., Sallie TeSelle, *Speaking in Parables* (Philadelphia: Fortress Press, 1975), p. 79. Also see Madeleine Boucher, *The Mysterious Parable: A Literary Study* (Washington: Catholic Biblical Association of America, 1977), pp. 20–21, in which the parable as extended metaphor has been equated with allegory. The understanding of metaphor and allegory in Boucher's work is confused and simplistic (cf. Chapter I, note 41). She defines metaphor, using rhetorical handbooks and dictionaries of literary terms, as a classical trope, but then perceives no difficulty in talking about it as an extended narrative (which she further confounds by calling the whole system allegory). Cf. Ricoeur, *La métaphore,* pp. 63–86.

34. TeSelle, pp. 71–72. The concept of the text interpreting the interpreter gained wide acceptance through its use by the "new hermeneuts" who followed and popularized the work of Ernst Fuchs and Gerhard Ebeling. For a critique of this movement as it related specifically to the parables see Norman Perrin, *Jesus and the Language of the Kingdom* (Philadelphia: Fortress Press, 1976), pp. 107–27.

35. Ibid., p. 77.

36. Ibid., pp. 78–79 (italics hers). Also cf. John Dominic Crossan, *In Parables: The Challenge of the Historical Jesus* (New York: Harper & Row, 1973), pp. 33, 55, 65–66, et al. Though I am personally impressed by Crossan's development of such concepts as historicity and temporality in the eschatology of the historical Jesus, his comments on the parable stories themselves often tend to become rather inflated and exaggerated.

37. It is not, however, difficult to find examples of the opposite response. For instance, in a recent interview in the *New York Times* Book Review section author Joan Didion, in explaining why she no longer attended church, said: "I stopped going to church because I hated the stories. You know the story about the prodigal son? I have never understood that story. I have never understood why the prodigal son should be treated any better than the other son. I have missed the point of a lot of parables." In "A Visit With Joan Didion," by Sara Davidson, *New York Times*, 3 April 1977, Sec. 7, pp. 37–38.

38. This statement is true even of those parables which begin with the formula "The kingdom of God is like . . . ," for although the lesser known element is named, the vagueness and ambiguity of the symbol Kingdom of God itself is such that its addition to the narrative sheds little light on the comparison being drawn. Also cf. Ricoeur, *La métaphore*, pp. 35–36, in which he, following Aristotle, views comparison as a metaphor rather than metaphor as a comparison.

39. Wheelwright, *Metaphor*, pp. 70–91. The discussion of epiphor and diaphor which follows comes essentially from this section of the book. Cf. Ricoeur's discussion and evaluation of Wheelwright in *La métaphore*, pp. 315–16.

40. Wheelwright, *Metaphor*, p. 72.

41. Ibid., p. 74. Cf. Ricoeur's defense of resemblance in *La métaphore*, pp. 245–50.

42. For Ricoeur, however, a metaphor in and of itself demands speculative discourse, whether the tenor is present or not. See *La métaphore*, pp. 380–84.

43. As cited in Wheelwright, *Metaphor*, p. 79.

44. Ibid., p. 78.

45. Ibid., p. 84.

46. Ibid., p. 85.

47. Robert Funk, *Language, Hermeneutic, and the Word of God* (New York: Harper & Row, 1966), p. 151.

CHAPTER III:
Parables In the Gospels and Out

1. Note much the same situation in Philostratus's *Vita Apollonii*, as discussed in Jonathan Z. Smith, "Good News Is No News: Aretalogy and the Gospel" in *Christianity, Judaism and Other Greco-Roman Cults: Studies for Morton Smith at Sixty*, ed. Jacob Neusner, Part 1 (Leiden: E. J. Brill, 1975), pp. 25–26.

2. See, e.g., the classic work of Siegfried Goebel, *The Parables of Jesus: A Methodical Exposition*, trans. Professor Banks (Edinburgh: T & T Clark, 1890), in which questions of interpretation are referred to the comments of Jesus within the gospel context.

3. The figure of a widow is certainly a paradigm for powerlessness in the society of the Ancient Near East (see, e.g., Joachim Jeremias, *The Parables of Jesus*, trans. S. H. Hooke [London: SCM Press; New York: Scribner's, 1972], p. 153). Whether in this particular story she should also be described as weak or helpless is questionable. The Greek word *(hypōpiazę̄)* which is translated by the

RSV as "wear out" actually carries the connotation of *bodily* harm (even in 1 Cor. 9:27, its only other use in the New Testament). It comes from *hypōpion* which means "to strike under the eye," or "to beat black and blue." A better translation of this phrase in Luke 18:5c would be "lest at last she come and beat me black and blue." What the unjust judge confesses himself to fear from the widow is no less than bodily assault. Whether the judge's fear is a statement of irony, hyperbole, or reasonable expectation is a matter for interpretation.

4. Rudolf Bultmann also pointed out the effect that a particular context had upon a saying of Jesus or a similitude, noting that simply by placing a saying within a certain context the evangelist suggested its interpretation. *History of the Synoptic Tradition,* trans. John Marsh (New York: Harper & Row, 1963), pp. 94–96, 193–94.

Throughout this chapter and the next a distinction is being drawn between the context into which a parable is placed and the final interpretation of it. Though the line between what is context and what is interpretation is not always definite and clear-cut, the point of the distinction is to stress that the interpretation of any parable involves three interacting elements: the parable story itself, the context into which it is placed, and the personal insight, sensitivity, and creativity of the individual interpreter. It is this last element that makes interpretation ultimately an art and not a technology. For a further discussion of this see Chapter IV.

5. See, e.g., C. H. Dodd, *The Parables of the Kingdom,* 3rd ed. (New York: Scribner's, 1961), pp. 14, 16–17.

6. It is of course often possible to suggest with some clarity what a parable may have meant for each individual evangelist as Jack Dean Kingsbury's *The Parables of Jesus in Matthew 13: A Study in Redaction-Criticism* (Richmond: John Knox Press, 1969) and Charles E. Carlston's *The Parables of the Triple Tradition* (Philadelphia: Fortress Press, 1975) attempt to do.

7. Jeremias, p. 133. Also cf. Norman Perrin, *Rediscovering the Teachings of Jesus* (New York: Harper & Row, 1967), pp. 99–101.

8. It is for this reason that one shies away from describing the parables as linguistic significations of events that take place or can take place in extra-linguistic reality, as Wittig suggests in the semiotic model. See Chapter II, n. 14. For a further discussion of "realism" in the parables see Chapter IV.

9. Other parables that contain elements that run counter to the cultural milieu or common sense would be, for example, the Doorkeeper in Luke 12:36–38 or the Wicked Tenants in Matt. 21:33–41/Mark 12:1–9/Luke 20:9–16. Jeremias has suggested that the details in these parables which seem contrary to the real Palestinian situation are allegorical elements added by the early church (see Jeremias, pp. 53, 70–73).

10. See, e.g., Jeremias, p. 134, and Robert Grant and David N. Freedman, *The Secret Sayings of Jesus* (New York: Doubleday & Company, Inc., 1960), pp. 192–93.

11. For some possible theological reasons for the alterations in the parable see Bertil Gärtner, *Theology of the Gospel According to Thomas,* trans. E. Sharpe (New York: Harper & Row, 1961), pp. 234 ff.

12. The synoptic parables also appearing in the Gospel of Thomas are as follows: the Sower (82:3-13), the Mustard Seed (84:26–33), the Thief (85:7–10 and 98:6–10), the Tares Among the Wheat (90:32—91:7), the Rich Fool (92:3–10), the Great Supper (92:10–35), the Wicked Tenants (93:1–16), the Pearl (94:14–18), the Leaven (97:2–6), the Lost Sheep (98:22–27), and the Treasure (98:31—99:3).

13. See, e.g., Jack T. Sanders, "Tradition and Redaction in Luke 15:11–32," *New Testament Studies* 15 (1969): 433–38.

14. Bultmann, p. 196. Bultmann, however, does think that the second episode is an original part of the parable.

15. See, e.g., Dan O. Via, Jr., *The Parables: Their Literary and Existential Dimension* (Philadelphia: Fortress Press, 1967), p. 167; Eta Linnemann, *Jesus of the Parables,* trans. John Sturdy (New York: Harper & Row, 1966), pp. 78–81; and Jeremias, pp. 131–32.

16. See Chapter V for a further discussion of the Prodigal Son and a suggestion for a more comprehensive interpretation of it.

17. This particular pericope concerning the exalted and the humbled in Luke 18:14 is far more appropriate in its other setting in Luke 14:11.

18. Cf. John Dominic Crossan's discussion of this inconsistency in *In Parables: The Challenge of the Historical Jesus* (New York: Harper & Row, 1973), pp. 59–62.

19. Ibid., p. 59.

20. Jeremias, p. 35.

21. The reversal of order does have a point, as Jeremias notes, for paying the last first ensures that the first hired will witness the generosity shown to the last hired. See Jeremias, pp. 35–36.

22. Crossan, pp. 81–82.

23. Much scholarly research has been done in this area; see, e.g., Kingsbury, and Theodore J. Weeden, *Mark: Traditions in Conflict* (Philadelphia: Fortress Press, 1971).

24. Augustine, *Confessions* 6.4; and cf. also 5.14.

25. A. M. Hunter, *Interpreting the Parables* (Philadelphia: Westminster Press, 1960), p. 27. See also Hunter's discussion of Luther's use of the allegorical method, by which he was able to find the notion of justification by faith everywhere, pp. 31–33.

26. Beryl Smalley, *The Study of the Bible in the Middle Ages* (Notre Dame: University of Notre Dame Press, 1964), p. 20. Also note her discussion of the war between the Antiochene and Alexandrian schools of biblical interpretation, with the victory going to Alexandria, pp. 6–20.

27. Cf. Smalley's discussion of allegory and history, pp. 2–4.

28. Jeremias, p. 114; Crossan, pp. 4–7.

29. Even in Crossan's reconstruction of the message of the historical Jesus he finds it necessary to build a bridge to Jesus' understanding of temporality and eschatology. That bridge is the conception of ontological time in the philosophy of Martin Heidegger—very much a twentieth-century view. Crossan, pp. 31–36.

30. The emphasis on canon here is not on the process of canonization but on the fact of canonization and its implications for interpretation. On the process of canonization see, e.g., Hans von Campenhausen, *The Formation of the Christian Bible,* trans. J. A. Baker (Philadelphia: Fortress Press, 1972); David L. Dungan, "The New Testament Canon in Recent Study," *Interpretation* 29 (October 1975): 339–51; Albert C. Sundberg, Jr., "The Bible Canon and the Christian Doctrine of Inspiration," *Interpretation* 29 (October 1975): 352–71.

31. An excellent modern example of this process would be "The Protestant Hour, United Methodist Series," radio sermons in August through November of 1974. Bishop W. Kenneth Goodson each week chose one parable to discuss in relation to the issues of contemporary life. (The sermons are reprinted by the Joint Communications Committee, United Methodist Church, 159 Forrest Avenue, N.E., Atlanta, Georgia.)

CHAPTER IV:
Guidelines for Interpretation

1. See, e.g., C. H. Dodd, *The Parables of the Kingdom,* 3rd ed. (New York: Harper & Row, 1973), pp. 159–63; Joachim Jeremias, *The Parables of Jesus,* trans. S. H. Hooke (London: SCM Press; New York: Scribner's, 1972), pp. 21–22; Sallie TeSelle, *Speaking in Parables* (Philadelphia: Fortress Press, 1975), pp. 71, 74–75.

2. Cf. this statement by Wolfgang Iser on the reader's relation to a syntactically indeterminate text: "Every literary text invites some form of participation on the part of the reader. A text which lays things out before the reader in such a way that he can either accept or reject them will lessen the degree of participation as it allows him nothing but a yes or no. Texts with such minimal indeterminacy tend to be tedious, for it is only when the reader is given the chance to participate actively that he will regard the text, whose intention he himself has helped to compose, as real. For we generally tend to regard things that we have made ourselves as being real. And so it can be said that indeterminacy is the fundamental precondition for reader participation." "Indeterminacy and the Reader's Response" in *Aspects of Narrative,* ed. J. Hillis Miller (New York: Columbia University Press, 1971), pp. 13–14. We have argued, with Susan Wittig, that the parables are not only syntactically indeterminate but semantically indeterminate as well. Cf. Iser, *The Implied Reader* (Baltimore: Johns Hopkins University Press, 1974).

3. Wittig, "A Theory of Multiple Meanings," *Semeia* 9 (1977): 88–89.

4. Cf. Rudolf Bultmann's development of the relationship between understanding (*Verständnis*) and preunderstanding (*Vorverständnis*) in interpretation, in "Das Problem der Hermeneutik," *Glauben und Verstehen* (Tübingen: J.C.B. Mohr, 1961), 2:216–22.

5. Wittig, p. 97.

6. See, e.g., Eduard Lohse, *The New Testament Environment,* trans. John E. Steely (Nashville: Abingdon, 1976); C. K. Barrett, *The New Testament Background: Selected Documents* (New York: Harper & Row, 1956); Bo Reicke, *The New Testament Era,* trans. David Green (Philadelphia: Fortress Press, 1968); Moses Hadas, *Hellenistic Culture* (New York: W. W. Norton & Company, 1959).

7. Iser, "Indeterminacy," p. 5. Cf. also Paul Ricoeur, *Interpretation Theory* (Fort Worth: Texas Christian University Press, 1976), p. 75: "The text is mute. An asymmetric relation obtains between text and reader, in which only one of the partners speaks for the two. The text is like a musical score and the reader like the orchestra conductor who obeys the instructions of the notation."

8. It is belief in the inseparability of form and content, and therefore the bonding of form to meaning, that keeps me unconvinced by E. D. Hirsch's arguments for hermeneutics as a logic of validation (in *Validity in Interpretation* [New Haven: Yale University Press, 1967]). Hirsch's basic distinction between the verbal meaning of a literary work and its continuing significance seems to suggest that "significance" is free of form, in that one changes while the other does not. See the discussion of Hirsch in Palmer, *Hermeneutics* (Evanston: Northwestern University Press, 1969), pp. 63–65; Iser, "Indeterminacy," pp. 4–5; and Ricoeur, "Construing and Constructing," *London Times Literary Supplement,* 25 February 1977, p. 216.

9. This concern with articulating the formal structure of the text was the impetus behind rhetorical criticism as formulated by James Muilenburg: "What I am interested in, above all, is in understanding the nature of Hebrew literary composition, in exhibiting the structural patterns that are employed for the

fashioning of a literary unit, whether in poetry or in prose, and in discerning the many and various devices by which the predications are formulated and ordered into a unified whole. Such an enterprise I should describe as rhetoric and the methodology as rhetorical criticism." "Form Criticism and Beyond," *Journal of Biblical Literature* 88 (March 1969): 8.

10. See the discussion in Chapter I of Jeremias's reconstruction of *Ur*-parable texts. Also cf. David Robertson's first three points concerning the literary study of biblical material in "Literature, the Bible As," *IDB Supplement* (Nashville: Abingdon, 1976), p. 548, and Brevard Childs's emphasis upon the text in its final form rather than in hypothetical reconstructions, in *The Book of Exodus* (Philadelphia: Westminster Press, 1974), pp. xiv–xv and passim.

11. Ricoeur, "Biblical Hermeneutics," *Semeia* 4 (1975): 65.

12. Ibid., p. 71.

13. Jonathan Culler, *Structuralist Poetics* (Ithaca: Cornell University Press, 1975), p. 31.

14. Ricoeur, "Biblical Hermeneutics," p. 65. Ricoeur goes on to argue that structural analysis can be "disconnected" from the ideology of structuralism and then "connected to existential interpretation." While one may be sympathetic to Ricoeur's intention of salvaging structural analysis for hermeneutics, it is difficult to find deep structural analyses that have successfully opened the way for a hermeneutical development of the message in a manner not available through other less cumbersome and less ideologically troublesome methodologies. For example in the recent book by Daniel Patte *What is Structural Exegesis?* (Philadelphia: Fortress Press, 1976), the parable of the Good Samaritan is examined in both a narrative structural analysis and a mythical structural analysis. After over twenty pages of charts, tables, equations, and graphs, Patte presents these "mere suggestions of the promising exegetical and hermeneutical results we can expect from structural analyses of the Bible": "The parable was proposed as a paradigm for discovering the 'signs of the kingdom.' When one can discover, in the concrete situation in which he lives, a 'good Samaritan,' one is in the presence of a manifestation of the mysterious kingly activity of God. Yet this identification of the 'good Samaritans' must be performed and verified with great care. There are many people performing good deeds who are not 'Samaritans' (indeed, the 'priests' and 'Levites' certainly perform good deeds). In order to fulfill the paradigm of the parable, the 'new story' must present a similar actualization of the narrative and mythical structures" (p. 83).

Surely John Dominic Crossan's conclusions concerning the Good Samaritan in *In Parables: The Challenge of the Historical Jesus* (New York: Harper & Row, 1973) are far more exciting and "promising" from the standpoint of exegetical and hermeneutical concerns: "The whole thrust of the story demands that one say what cannot be said, what is a contradiction in terms: Good + Samaritan. On the lips of the historical Jesus the story demands that the hearer respond by saying the contradictory, the impossible, the unspeakable. . . . But when good (clerics) and bad (Samaritan) become, respectively, bad and good, a world is being challenged and we are faced with polar reversal" (p. 64). Crossan arrived at his conclusions after about nine pages of historical- and literary-critical arguments rather than twenty pages of equations and tables. Not only are the hermeneutical results of most structural analyses extremely scanty and equally available from studies using other methodologies, but also the length and complexity of such analyses are such that the pragmatic critic often feels called upon to invoke Ockham's razor against the whole enterprise. Since the methodology is still in the process of developing, it is possible that future structural analyses will prove helpful to the task of hermeneutics. If so, then the methodology will need to be included among the interpreter's skills. Until or unless that usefulness is shown, however, structural analysis will remain a hermeneutical dead end, the exploration of codes, not messages. For further discussions of structuralism and biblical studies see the articles in *Interpretation* 28 (April 1974), and for further expressions of dissatisfaction concerning structural exegesis see Daniel Patte, ed., *Semiology and the Parables* (Pittsburgh: The Pickwick Press, 1976), pp. 68, 157, 173, 187–88.

15. The messages a story may bear are not at all related necessarily to the author's intention. One problem apparent in Daniel Patte's book (*Structural Exegesis?* pp. 9–16) is his statement that texts can be studied as reflections either of what the author intended or of what the linguistic, narrative, and mythical structures imposed upon the author. Following that formula he classifies all textual studies as either historical (what the author meant) or structural. He leaves no room for this kind of literary study in which the focus is upon the various meanings or messages a text may have in different interpretive systems. The author's intention, in fact, may have little or no effect on the meaning of a work. As Ricoeur notes, "His [the author's] intention is often unknown to us, sometimes redundant, sometimes useless, and sometimes even harmful as regards the interpretation of the verbal meaning of his work." *Interpretation Theory*, p. 76.

16. Leon Golden, trans., *Aristotle's Poetics*, commentary by O. B. Hardison (Englewood Cliffs: Prentice-Hall, 1968), p. 6.

17. Bultmann, p. 191. Bultmann has some textual support for his assertion that the son who says no but eventually goes should come last in the story. The parable of the Two Sons presents a difficult text-critical problem because there are three relatively well supported variant traditions of it. (See Bruce M. Metzger, *A Textual Commentary on the Greek New Testament* [New York: United Bible Societies, 1971], pp. 55–56.) I support the version chosen by the Editorial Committee of the United Bible Societies both because I think the textual tradition is stronger and because the integrity of this version is enforced by the formal patterning of the story. The law of end stress which Bultmann cites can be helpful if it is not used as an absolute criterion. Each parable must be judged primarily on the basis of its own internal structuring.

18. See, e.g., Monroe C. Beardsley, "Style and Good Style," pp. 3–15; Richard Ohmann, "Literature as Sentences," pp. 149–57; and Ian Watt, "The First Paragraph of *The Ambassadors:* An Explication," pp. 266–83, all in Glen A. Love and Michael Payne, eds., *Contemporary Essays on Style* (Glenview: Scott, Foresman and Company, 1969).

19. Muilenburg's introduction to rhetorical criticism appeared in his article "Form Criticism and Beyond." Excellent recent examples of the methodology can be seen in Phyllis Trible, "Wisdom Builds a Poem: The Architecture of Proverbs 1:20–33," *Journal of Biblical Literature* 94 (December 1975): 509–18 and Trible, "The Gift of a Poem: A Rhetorical Study of Jeremiah 31: 15–22," *Andover Newton Quarterly* 17 (March 1977): 271–80.

20. Muilenburg, p. 10.

21. Ibid., p. 17. Cf. also Muilenburg, "A Study in Hebrew Rhetoric: Repetition and Style," *Congress Volume, Vetus Testamentum* Supplement, No. 1 (Leiden: Brill, 1953), pp. 97–111.

22. This particular section of Mark 4 is extremely interesting in terms of rhetorical patterns. Though we will discuss below the two parables found in vv. 26–32, parallel repetitions also dominate the section immediately preceding the two parables, vv. 21–25.

23. One of the first discussions of the use of chiastic patterns within the New Testament is found in Nils W. Lund, *Chiasmus in the New Testament* (Chapel Hill: University of North Carolina Press, 1942). A major part of Lund's study relates to the use of chiastic motif structures rather than chiastically repeated words and phrases. Since the judgment as to what constitutes a motif and what does not often becomes a highly subjective decision, I insist upon the presence of exact word or phrase repetitions in determining the existence of these parallel or chiastic patterns. This point will be discussed further below.

24. See Trible, "Wisdom," pp. 513–14.

25. Variations of an exact word or phrase can appear in at least three different ways:

1. Grammatical variations—in Greek a change of case or tense often involves alterations in the formation of the word itself; e.g., in Luke 18:3, *ekdikēson*, "vindicate," but in Luke 18:5, *ekdikēsō*.
2. Nominalizations—in Greek, as in English, related verbs, nouns, and adjectives often use the same basic forms; e.g., in English, *to dance* and *dancer, to employ* and *employer, employee;* in Greek, *chairō*, "rejoice," and *chara*, "joy," or *lychnia*, "lampstand," and *lychnos*, "lamp."
3. Word combinations—in Greek many related words are formed by the combination of other words with them (e.g., in Luke 16:4 both *oikos* and *oikonomos* appear, "the home" and "the home-tender" or "steward"); word combinations are particularly common in Greek verbs, which are often given various nuances by prefixing prepositions to the basic verbal form, e.g., *erchomai*, "go," and *eiserchomai*, "go in or enter," and *exerchomai*, "go out or come out."

26. Kenneth E. Bailey, *Poet and Peasant: A Literary-Cultural Approach to the Parables in Luke* (Grand Rapids: Eerdmans Publishing Co., 1976), p. 65.

27. Ibid., pp. 72–73, 95, 120, 159–61, 191.

28. Ibid., pp. 72–74.

29. Crossan, pp. 96–120. See also Ricoeur's views on the clustering of parables, in "Biblical Hermeneutics," pp. 100–101.

30. Crossan, pp. 115–20.

31. Donald R. Fletcher, "The Riddle of the Unjust Steward: Is Irony the Key?" *Journal of Biblical Literature* 82 (March 1963): 15–30.

32. Francis E. Williams, "Is Almsgiving the Point of the 'Unjust Steward'?" *Journal of Biblical Literature* 83 (September 1964): 293–97.

33. Dan O. Via, Jr., *The Parables: Their Literary and Existential Dimension* (Philadelphia: Fortress Press, 1967), pp. 159-61.

34. I have chosen the version of the parable of the Wicked Tenants found in the Gospel of Mark mainly because of the chiastic and parallel repetition patterns it presents. This version has been criticized for the direct quotation from the LXX rendition of Isa. 5:2 in v. 1. This quotation has been said to indicate Mark's allegorizing tendencies in the parable. While I do not reject the quotation, I am inclined to see it as an addition to the text, not however because it represents allegory, but rather because it is not *used* any further in a text-form that is distinguished by its economy of description.

35. Contra Crossan, pp. 109–10 and 90–96.

36. Bultmann, pp. 182–84.

37. See the thorough discussion in Via, pp. 96–107.

38. Dodd, p. 9.

39. Of course, it was a literary critic who first described the realistic tone of many biblical stories. Erich Auerbach in fact suggested that the Bible was one

of the foundations of Western literary realism. *Mimesis,* trans. Willard R. Trask (Princeton: Princeton University Press, 1953), pp. 7–23, 40–49.

40. Ricoeur, "Biblical Hermeneutics," pp. 99–100. Cf. Via, pp. 105–6.

41. Jeremias, p. 30.

42. For a discussion of the mustard seed's comparison with the cedars of Lebanon see Robert Funk, "The Looking-Glass Tree Is for the Birds," *Interpretation* 27 (January 1973): 3–9.

43. Jeremias, p. 147.

44. Ibid., p. 30.

45. Robert Scholes and Robert Kellogg, *The Nature of Narrative* (London: Oxford University Press, 1966), p. 84.

46. Ibid., p. 204.

47. Ibid.

48. Ibid., p. 89.

CHAPTER V:
Example: The Parable of the Prodigal Son

1. Simon O. Lesser, a literary critic who uses psychoanalytic concepts well, has expressed the fear of many critics opposed to such criticism in this way: "The cry of 'reduction' is immediately raised. Vigorous and sometimes angry voices are to be heard protesting that literature should not be assimilated to psychology, or economics or sociology. . . . The things that distinguish literature as literature seem peculiarly difficult to isolate and focus upon; it seems easier to discuss almost anything else. Thus there is a very real danger that a novel, for example, may be treated as though it were a kind of case history, as though only its meaning mattered, or that it will be used to document some economic development or cultural trend. It is probably safe to say that most discussion of literature assimilates it to something else. In extreme cases, a body of knowledge first introduced to explicate literature may end by claiming the center of the stage. Literature is relegated to a supporting role; it does not so much speak as stand by to be pointed to when it can be of service in illustrating a statement about something else." Lesser, *Fiction and the Unconscious* (New York: Random House, 1957), p. 294.

All interpretations of a polyvalent text must of necessity involve reductionism, for choosing one meaning for a text capable of multiple meanings reduces the potential of the text. As long as the interpreter realizes that he or she has actualized only one of the many possibilities the text contains, then this unavoidable reductionism is not deadly. The serious cry of reductionism should be raised against any interpretation that insists a polyvalent text means in one way and only one way.

2. Actually, good psychoanalytic practice and good literary criticism are not very far apart. As the literary critic Edward Wasiolek has said, "A good Freudian for me acknowledges difficulties, sees complexities, and sees limitations" (in letter received by author 3 June 1975). Good literary criticism and good Freudian practice are both tentative arts, requiring a light touch that attempts not to strain or push categories beyond the suggestive or the insightful. In the Freudian interpretations that follow, I have purposely not forced every idea to its limit or insisted that every formal element in the story correspond to some aspect of psychoanalytic thought: such an endeavor would be both poor literary criticism and poor Freudian theory.

3. Rudolf Bultmann, *History of the Synoptic Tradition,* trans. John Marsh (New York: Harper & Row, 1963), p. 196.

4. Dan O. Via, Jr., *The Parables: Their Literary and Existential Dimension* (Philadelphia: Fortress Press, 1967), p. 167.

5. Georges Crespy discusses the oedipal nature of the parable in his "Psychanalyse et Foi" in *Essais sur la situation actuelle de la foi* (Paris: Les editions du Cerf, 1970), pp. 41–56.

6. Sigmund Freud, *On Dreams* (New York: W. W. Norton & Company, Inc., 1952), p. 50. For a further discussion of this topic see *The Interpretation of Dreams* (New York: Avon, 1965), pp. 344–74.

7. Freud, *On Dreams,* pp. 37–41. Cf. Freud's own analysis of literature in relation to day-dreaming in "The Relation of the Poet to Day-Dreaming," *On Creativity and the Unconscious,* selected with introduction by Benjamin Nelson (New York: Harper & Row, 1958), pp. 44–54.

8. Freud, *On Dreams,* pp. 62–63.

9. This further meaning for *bios* is reinforced by its use elsewhere in the gospels. It is the word used of the widow's mite in Mark 12:44/Luke 21:4. She is praised by Jesus for giving all of her "living." A similar use of *bios* is found in the *varia lectio* of Luke 8:43: The woman with the flow of blood has spent all of her "living" on physicians for twelve years. Not only her money, but also the entire concern, vitality, and substance of her life for twelve years has been spent in an effort to relieve her constant suffering. In fact *bios* is used only once in the gospels without this further connotation of the whole substance and course of life (viz. Luke 8:14).

10. Some scholars have taken only the last part of this final speech, v. 32, to be its entirety (cf. Via, p. 167). Yet the text clearly shows that the father's final speech begins in v. 31 with *"ho de eipen autǭ, teknon, . . ."* and continues to the end of v. 32. The whole of the father's response, and not just half of it, receives the end stress of the narrative.

11. Bultmann, p. 196.

12. Paul Tillich, *The Shaking of the Foundations* (New York: Charles Scribner's Sons, 1948), p. 163.

13. Freud, *The Ego and the Id,* trans. Joan Riviere (New York: W. W. Norton & Company, Inc., 1960), p. 46.

14. Ibid., p. 35.

15. Ibid., pp. 45–46.

16. Joachim Jeremias, *The Parables of Jesus,* trans. S. H. Hooke (London: SCM Press; New York: Scribner's, 1972), p. 128.

17. C. H. Dodd, *The Parables of the Kingdom,* 3rd ed. (New York: Scribner's, 1961), pp. 92–93.

18. Jeremias, p. 130.

19. Freud, "Instincts and Their Vicissitudes" in *General Psychological Theory,* ed. Philip Rieff (New York: Collier Books, 1963), p. 97.

20. Freud, *Totem and Taboo,* trans. James Strachey (New York: W. W. Norton & Company, Inc., 1950), p. 60.

21. Freud, *Civilization and its Discontents,* trans. Joan Riviere (New York: Doubleday and Company, Inc., n.d.), pp. 70–71.

22. Freud, "Instincts," pp. 100, 103. For a further discussion of the development of ambivalence and its relation to the oedipal period see Freud, *Group Psychology and the Analysis of the Ego,* trans. James Strachey (New York: W. W. Norton & Company, Inc., 1959), pp. 37–42.

23. Freud, *Totem and Taboo,* p. 49.

24. Ibid., p. 70.

25. Ibid., p. 72.

26. For a discussion of Freud vs. the Freudian revisionists see Herbert Marcuse, *Eros and Civilization* (Boston: Beacon Press, 1955), pp. 238–74. For some recent discussions of Freudianism and contemporary issues see, e.g., Jean Miller, ed., *Psychoanalysis and Women* (Baltimore: Penguin Books, 1973) and Hendrik Ruitenbeek, ed., *Psychoanalysis and Existential Philosophy* (New York: E. P. Dutton & Co., Inc., 1962). For a current scientific evaluation of Freud see Seymour Fisher and Roger Greenberg, *The Scientific Credibility of Freud's Theories and Therapies* (New York: Basic Books, Inc., 1977).

27. Paul Ricoeur, *Interpretation Theory* (Fort Worth: Texas Christian University Press, 1976), p. 79. By using two closely akin interpretations, as I have done here, one heightens the contrasts between them and thus presents a pointed methodological illustration. One can of course go on to compare the probabilities of interpretations arising from quite different systems.

Selected Bibliography

ON THE PARABLES

Bailey, Kenneth E. *Poet and Peasant: A Literary-Cultural Approach to the Parables in Luke.* Grand Rapids: Eerdmans Publishing Co., 1976.

Boucher, Madeleine. *The Mysterious Parable: A Literary Study.* Washington: Catholic Biblical Association of America, 1977.

Carlston, Charles. "Changing Fashions in Interpreting the Parables." *Andover Newton Quarterly* 14 (1974): 227–33.

———. *The Parables of the Triple Tradition.* Philadelphia: Fortress Press, 1975.

Crespy, G. *Essais sur la situation actuelle de la foi.* Paris: Les editions du Cerf, 1970.

Crossan, John Dominic. *In Parables: The Challenge of the Historical Jesus.* New York: Harper & Row, 1973.

———. "Parable and Example in the Teaching of Jesus." *Semeia* 1 (1974): 63–104.

———. "Structuralist Analysis and the Parables of Jesus." *Semeia* 1 (1974): 192–221.

Dodd, C. H. *The Parables of the Kingdom.* 3rd ed. New York: Scribner's, 1961.

Fletcher, Donald. "The Riddle of the Unjust Steward: Is Irony the Key?" *Journal of Biblical Literature* 82 (1963): 15–30.

Funk, Robert. *Language, Hermeneutic, and the Word of God.* New York: Harper & Row, 1966.

———. "The Looking-Glass Tree Is for the Birds." *Interpretation* 27 (1973): 3–9.

Goebel, Siegfried. *The Parables of Jesus: A Methodical Exposition.* Translated by Professor Banks. Edinburgh: T & T Clark, 1890.

Hunter, A. M. *Interpreting the Parables.* Philadelphia: Westminster Press, 1960.

Jeremias, Joachim. *The Parables of Jesus.* Translated by S. H. Hooke. 3rd ed. London: SCM Press; New York: Scribner's, 1972.

Jones, G. V. *The Art and Truth of the Parables.* London: S.P.C.K., 1964.

Jülicher, Adolf. *Die Gleichnisreden Jesu.* 2 vols. Tübingen: J. C. B. Mohr (Paul Siebeck), vol. 1 1888,

2d ed. 1899; vol. 2 1899, 2d ed. 1910.

Kingsbury, Jack D. "Ernst Fuchs' Existentialist Interpretation of the Parables." *Lutheran Quarterly* 22 (1970): 380–95.

———. "The Parables of Jesus in Current Research." *Dialog* 11 (1972): 101–7.

———. *The Parables of Jesus in Matthew 13: A Study in Redaction-Criticism.* Richmond: John Knox Press, 1969.

Linnemann, Eta. *Jesus of the Parables.* Translated by John Sturdy. New York: Harper & Row, 1966.

Marxsen, Willie. "Redaktionsgeschichtliche Erklärung der sogenannten Parabeltheorie des Markus." *Zeitschrift für Theologie und Kirche* 52 (1955): 255–71.

Patte, Daniel, ed. *Semiology and the Parables.* Pittsburgh: The Pickwick Press, 1976.

Perrin, Norman. *Jesus and the Language of the Kingdom.* Philadelphia: Fortress Press, 1976.

Petersen, Norman. "On the Notion of Genre in Via's 'Parable and Example Story: A Literary-Structuralist Approach.'" *Semeia* 1 (1974): 134–81.

Sanders, Jack T. "Tradition and Redaction in Luke 15:11–32." *New Testament Studies* 15 (1969): 433–38.

Scott, Bernard B. "The Prodigal Son: A Structuralist Interpretation." *Semeia* 9 (1977): 45–73.

TeSelle, Sallie. *Speaking in Parables.* Philadelphia: Fortress Press, 1975.

Tolbert, Mary Ann. "The Prodigal Son: An Essay in Literary Criticism from a Psychoanalytic Perspective." *Semeia* 9 (1977): 1–20.

Via, Dan O., Jr. "Parable and Example Story: A Literary-Structuralist Approach." *Semeia* 1 (1974): 105–33.

———. *The Parables: Their Literary and Existential Dimension.* Philadelphia: Fortress Press, 1967.

———. "The Prodigal Son: A Jungian Reading." *Semeia* 9 (1977): 21–43.

Wilkens, W. "Die Redaktion des Gleichniskapitels Mark 4 durch Matth." *Theologische Zeitschrift* 20 (1964): 304–27.

Williams, Francis E. "Is Almsgiving the Point of the 'Unjust Steward'?" *Journal of Biblical Literature* 83 (1964): 293–97.

Wittig, Susan. "A Theory of Multiple Meanings." *Semeia* 9 (1977): 75–103.

ON LITERARY AND HERMENEUTICAL STUDIES

Auerbach, Erich. *Mimesis.* Translated by Willard R. Trask. Princeton: Princeton University Press, 1953.

Barthes, Roland. *Elements of Semiology.* Translated by Annette Lavers and Colin Smith. Boston: Beacon Press, 1967.

———. *Mythologies.* Translated by

Annette Lavers. New York: Hill and Wang, 1972.

Berggren, Douglas. "The Use and Abuse of Metaphor." *The Review of Metaphysics* 16 (1962–63): 237–58 and 450–72.

Black, Max. *Models and Metaphors.* Ithaca: Cornell University Press, 1962.

Bloomfield, Morton. "Allegory as Interpretation." *New Literary History* 3 (1972): 301–17.

Booth, Wayne. *The Rhetoric of Fiction.* Chicago: University of Chicago Press, 1961.

————. *A Rhetoric of Irony.* Chicago: University of Chicago Press, 1974.

Bultmann, Rudolf. "Das Problem der Hermeneutik." *Glauben und Verstehen* 2:211–35. Tübingen: J.C.B. Mohr, 1961.

Culler, Jonathan. *Structuralist Poetics.* Ithaca: Cornell University Press, 1975.

Fletcher, Angus. *Allegory: The Theory of a Symbolic Mode.* Ithaca: Cornell University Press, 1964.

Golden, Leon, trans. *Aristotle's Poetics.* Commentary by O. B. Hardison. Englewood Cliffs: Prentice-Hall, 1968.

Greimas, A.-J. *Sémantique structural: Recherche de méthode.* Paris: Larousse, 1966.

Hirsch, E. D. *Validity in Interpretation.* New Haven: Yale University Press, 1967.

Iser, Wolfgang. *The Implied Reader.* Baltimore: Johns Hopkins University Press, 1974.

Lesser, Simon O. *Fiction and the Unconscious.* New York: Random House, 1957.

Lewis, C. S. *Allegory of Love.* London: Oxford University Press, 1936.

Love, Glen A. and Payne, Michael, eds. *Contemporary Essays on Style.* Glenview: Scott, Foresman and Company, 1969.

Lund, Nils W. *Chiasmus in the New Testament.* Chapel Hill: University of North Carolina Press, 1942.

Miller, J. Hillis, ed. *Aspects of Narrative.* New York: Columbia University Press, 1971.

Muilenburg, James. "Form Criticism and Beyond." *Journal of Biblical Literature* 88 (March 1969): 1–18.

Murrin, Michael. *The Veil of Allegory.* Chicago: University of Chicago Press, 1969.

Palmer, Richard E. *Hermeneutics.* Evanston: Northwestern University Press, 1969.

Patte, Daniel. *What Is Structural Exegesis?* Philadelphia: Fortress Press, 1976.

Richards, I. A. *The Philosophy of Rhetoric.* London: Oxford University Press, 1936.

Ricoeur, Paul. "Biblical Hermeneutics." *Semeia* 4 (1975): 29–148.

————. *The Conflict of Interpretations.* Evanston: Northwestern University Press, 1974.

————. "Construing and Constructing." *London Times Literary Supplement*, 25 February 1977, p. 216.

———. *Interpretation Theory*. Fort Worth: Texas Christian University Press, 1976.

———. *La métaphore vive*. Paris: Editions du Seuil, 1975.

Saussure, Ferdinand. *Course in General Linguistics*. Edited by Charles Bally and Albert Sechehaye. New York: McGraw-Hill, 1959.

Scholes, Robert. *Structuralism in Literature*. New Haven: Yale University Press, 1974.

Scholes, Robert and Kellogg, Robert. *The Nature of Narrative*. London: Oxford University Press, 1966.

Trible, Phyllis. "Wisdom Builds a Poem: The Architecture of Proverbs 1:20–33." *Journal of Biblical Literature* 94 (December 1975): 509–18.

Wheelwright, Philip. *The Burning Fountain*. Bloomington: Indiana University Press, 1968.

———. *Metaphor and Reality*. Bloomington: Indiana University Press, 1962.

Wilder, Amos. *Early Christian Rhetoric: The Language of the Gospel*, 1964. Rev. ed. Cambridge: Harvard University Press, 1971.

Wimsatt, William K. and Brooks, Cleanth. *Literary Criticism: A Short History*. New York: Random House, 1957.

Wittig, Susan. "The Historical Development of Structuralism." *Soundings* 58 (1975): 1–22.

Indexes

AUTHORS

Aristotle, 74–75, 123, 125, 130
Auerbach, E., 131–32
Augustine, 63–64, 124, 127

Bailey, K. E., 22–23, 82, 118, 119, 131
Barrett, C. K., 128
Barthes, R., 35, 36, 122, 123
Berggren, D., 124
Black, M., 34, 40, 51, 122, 124
Bloomfield, M., 121
Booth, W., 124
Boucher, M., 118, 120, 124
Brooks, C., 124
Bultmann, R., 16, 58, 77, 86, 94, 117, 126, 127, 128, 130, 131, 132

Campenhausen, H. v., 127
Carlston, C., 21–22, 23, 118–19, 126
Childs, B., 129
Crespy, G., 133
Crossan, J. D., 15, 16–17, 20, 27–28, 29–30, 33, 48, 60, 62, 64, 83, 117, 118, 120, 121, 122, 125, 127, 129, 131
Culler, J., 40, 122, 123, 129

Dodd, C. H., 15, 23, 24–26, 40, 49, 62, 107, 117, 118, 119, 121, 124, 126, 128, 131, 133
Dungan, D. L., 127

Ferré, F., 122
Fisher, S., 134
Fletcher, A., 121
Fletcher, D., 131
Freud, S., 94, 95, 96, 102–13, 133–34

Funk, R., 20, 28, 49, 118, 121, 125, 132

Gärtner, B., 126
Greenberg, R., 134
Goebel, S., 125
Grant, R., 126
Greimas, A.-J., 30, 35, 122, 123

Hadas, M., 128
Hirsch, E. D., 120, 122, 128
Hunter, A. M., 64, 127

Iser, W., 128

Jeremias, J., 15, 19–20, 23, 24–27, 28, 48, 49, 56, 60, 62, 64, 89, 108, 117, 118, 119, 120, 121, 125, 126, 127, 128, 129, 132, 133
Jones, G. V., 15, 28–29, 119, 121
Jülicher, A., 16, 18, 23, 24, 27–28, 93, 115, 117, 118, 119, 120
Jüngel, E., 119, 120, 121

Kellogg, R., 90, 132
Kingsbury, J. D., 21–22, 118, 119, 121, 126, 127

Lesser, S. O., 132
Lewis, C. S., 121
Linnemann, E., 118, 121, 127
Lohse, E., 128
Lund, N. W., 131

Marcuse, H., 134
Marrou, H. I., 123–24
Marxsen, W., 118

Metzger, B. M., 130
Miller, J., 134
Muilenburg, J., 78, 124, 128–29, 130
Murrin, M., 121

Palmer, R. E., 120, 128
Patte, D., 129, 130
Perrin, N., 20, 117, 118, 119, 121, 122, 124, 126
Petersen, N., 117

Reicke, B., 128
Richards, I. A., 43, 124
Ricoeur, P., 14, 39–40, 73, 89, 112, 117, 120, 123, 124, 125, 128, 129, 130, 131, 132, 134
Robertson, D., 129
Robinson, J. M., 118

Sanders, J. T., 127
Saussure, F., 35–36, 122
Scholes, R., 90, 123, 132
Schweitzer, A., 118
Scott, B. B., 122
Smalley, B., 64, 127
Smith, J. Z., 125
Sundberg, A. C., 127

TeSelle, S., 41–42, 45, 124, 125, 128
Tillich, P., 105
Tolbert, M. A., 122
Tracy, D., 34, 122
Trible, P., 130, 131

Via, D. O., 15, 17, 20, 28–30, 33, 48, 95–96, 117, 118, 119, 121, 122, 123, 127, 131, 132, 133

Weeden, T. J., 127
Wheelwright, P., 41, 44–48, 124, 125
Wilder, A., 20, 28, 118, 121
Wilkens, W., 118
Williams, F. E., 131
Wimsatt, W. K., 124
Wittig, S., 35, 36–40, 45, 69, 70, 122, 123, 128

PARABLES

The Doorkeeper (Mark 13:34–36; Luke 12:36–38), 126
The Friend at Midnight (Luke 11:5–8), 24
The Good Samaritan (Luke 10:30–36), 16–17, 24, 29–30, 57, 59–60, 129
The Leaven (Matt. 13:33; Luke 13:20–21; Gos. of Thom. 97:2–6), 18, 90, 126
The Lost Coin (Luke 15:8–9), 16, 55, 57, 74
The Lost Sheep (Matt. 18:12–13; Luke 15:4–6; Gos. of Thom. 98:22–27), 16, 55–57, 126
The Mustard Seed (Matt. 13:31–32; Mark 4:30–32; Luke 13:18–19; Gos. of Thom. 84:26–33), 79–81, 90, 126
The Pearl (Matt. 13:45; Gos. of Thom. 94:14–18), 126
The Pharisee and the Publican (Luke 18:10–14), 57, 59, 74, 75–77
The Prodigal Son (Luke 15:11–32), 16, 28–29, 35, 57–58, 71, 74–75, 76, 90, 94–114, 127
The Rich Fool (Luke 12:16–20; Gos. of Thom. 92:3–10), 126
The Rich Man and Lazarus (Luke 16:19–31), 57, 61
The Seed Growing Secretly (Mark 4:26–29), 16, 25–26, 79–81
The Sower (Matt. 13:3–8; Mark 4:3–8; Luke 8:5–8; Gos. of Thom. 82:3–13), 67, 126
The Tares Among the Wheat (Matt. 13:24–30; Gos. of Thom. 90:32–91:7), 126
The Ten Maidens (Matt. 25:1–12), 57, 90
The Thief (Matt. 24:43–44, Luke 12:39–40; Gos. of Thom. 85:7–10; 98:6–10), 126
The Treasure (Matt. 13:44; Gos. of Thom. 98:31–99:3), 126

The Two Sons (Matt. 21:28–31), 74, 75–77

The Unjust Judge (Luke 18:2–5), 18, 52–53, 54, 57, 58, 81, 90

The Unjust Steward (Luke 16:1–8a), 57, 61, 74, 83–89

The Unmerciful Servant (Matt. 18:23–34), 57, 74, 90

The Wedding Feast (Great Supper) (Matt. 22:1–10; Luke 14:16–24; Gos. of Thom. 92:10–35), 41–42, 90, 126

The Wicked Tenants (Matt. 21:33–41; Mark 12:1–9; Luke 20:9–16; Gos. of Thom. 93:1–16), 74, 75, 83–89, 126, 131

The Workers in the Vineyard (Matt. 20:1–15), 24, 57, 60, 74, 76